S0-BZE-290

Whole Food, Bowl Food

Whole Food, Bowl Food

Naturally gluten free, delicious home cooking

ANNA LISLE

NEW HOLLAND

For Andrew

Contents

INTRODUCTION

I grew up in a home where sharing a meal was at the heart of our family. There was always something simmering on the stove or baking in the oven, filling the house with delicious aromas. As children, my brothers and I weren't fussy eaters and we didn't just eat food because we were given it, we were passionate about eating, devouring everything in our sight. We would beg Mum to cook us orange cakes, coconut slice and lasagna. It wasn't until I grew older that I realised that delicious food was the result of good cooking and I gravitated towards the kitchen. Our family live on a sheep and cattle property in rural Australia and it only really occurred to me much later in life that we ate from the garden and our meals were based around what we harvested. I haven't always been passionate about eating a diet rich in whole, natural foods because that is just the way I've always eaten. In many respects, I took it for granted and assumed that everyone ate the same. It is only now that I understand how my childhood has shaped my food philosophy and passion for eating whole, unprocessed foods.

The response from my first cookbook, *Bowl & Fork* was incredibly humbling and it made me realise that I wasn't alone in my love of bowl food. I found the process of developing and writing recipes incredibly rewarding and very soon after *Bowl & Fork* was published, I was back in the kitchen tinkering away with new ideas and concepts. Which brings me to *Whole Food, Bowl Food*—a collection of gluten free recipes that celebrates simple, nourishing food. There really is something so comforting about eating a meal in a bowl, isn't there? The way you can happily nurse a bowl on your lap and scoop up just the right amount of each component of the dish—a slice of this, a mound of leafy greens and a scrape of dressing—all while perched at the kitchen counter or curled up on the lounge. It is a nurturing and grounding way to enjoy food, that can be shared with others or solo.

I am hesitant to outline exactly what I consider whole foods to be, as the health and nutrition world is constantly evolving. However, for me, eating a whole food diet is simply to enjoy real food, that is, ingredients in their most natural state—whole grains, full fat dairy, lean meats, seafood, nuts, seeds, fruits and vegetables. Honest, unprocessed food, without hidden salts, sugar and additives. A large proportion of our society has a passive relationship with food—it enjoys eating it but is not necessarily interested in how or why the food got to their plate (or bowl, in this case). Eating a whole food diet encourages you to have a relationship with the food you're eating—it forces you to be in tune with the seasons. I don't ever want my recipes to be followed like a textbook, that's why I always encourage substitutions and variations. You need to cook food that works for you—you need to be able to source ingredients from your local markets, not imported from across the globe—and it needs to be affordable. In other words, I believe in keeping it real.

Regardless of what a dish entails, I believe that the notion of cooking for yourself and your family is a positive and rewarding act. For me and for many, it is the ultimate display of kindness and love. We have all heard about mindful eating but I am a believer of what British food personality, Nigella Lawson, describes as mindful cooking. Most days I find myself stressing about something or running from one thing to another, so, by the end of the day, my time in the kitchen is where I decompress and calm my mind. The simple act of chopping onions or picking through herbs—focusing on these seemingly mundane tasks—casts a sort of spell, a trance if you'd like, and forces me to live in the moment.

Halfway through writing this book, I moved to London with my husband, Andrew. I left Australia's sunshine, my tiny herb garden and my blooming kaffir lime tree all behind, setting up house in a little terrace in London's north. I didn't bring any of my kitchen appliances or utensils which, at the time, was quite horrifying, especially as I was frantically trying to test recipes. However, it has turned out to be a blessing. Not only did I discover how few pantry ingredients I use in my dishes but also that I didn't need a lot of the extra gadgets I had acquired over the years.

I believe it is in the spirit of the whole foods philosophy to avoid waste. I'm particularly frugal. I save even the tiniest spoonful of leftovers and I keep every carrot top and onion skin. I can thank my parents for that— 'waste not, want not' was a phrase drummed into me from a young age. Throughout the book, I've written a few pointers that may help you minimise your waste—like having a resealable bag in your freezer to keep any vegetable offcuts to make stock—but at the end of the day, I encourage common sense. I understand that in an ideal world, we would all forage for wild ingredients, churn our own butter and have our own chickens to collect our daily eggs, but for most of us the closest we get to that is foraging through our refrigerator. Instead of packing up our lives and moving to the countryside, we can make small changes simply through the types of food we choose to cook and eat—if you can view *Whole Food, Bowl Food* as a way in which to cut back the amount of processed foods you consume, through making a dish from scratch and sourcing fresh ingredients, then my job is done.

Ultimately, my favorite thing about working with food has been sharing my passion with others, whether it's by teaching cooking classes, through my cookbooks or simply by chatting to a stranger on the street. I love it when I'm sent a photo of a dish someone has made from *Bowl & Fork* or when someone tries a grain like millet for the first time and they decide to implement it into their diet.

I hope these recipes give you as much pleasure as they've given me and if you want to continue the conversation, find me on Instagram @annalisle.

MY WHOLE FOOD PHILOSOPHY

While I'm not coeliac, the recipes in *Whole Food, Bowl Food* are all gluten free, which is how I prefer to eat. I don't buy any gluten free products, which are generally highly processed. I cook naturally gluten free meals, using whole food ingredients. Rather than refined sugar, I enjoy Mother Nature's source of sugar—fruit—in abundance. I'm not afraid of fat—I eat plenty of extra virgin olive oil, nuts, seeds and full fat dairy.

However, please let me stress that I don't believe in setting up guidelines for others, I don't preach to everybody to follow this way of eating—it is important to find out what works for you. If a food makes you feel lousy, don't consume it. Whether it's wheat, kale, dairy or holy water—listen to your body. There is no one single lifestyle that will suit everyone—I believe in an intuitive eating philosophy. If you can tolerate wheat, feel free to adapt and change my recipes. I simply want my recipes to inspire you to cook and eat in a way that works for you and your family.

We live in a society that is very focused on how we can improve ourselves, from our minds to our bodies and I think some eating philosophies prey on this obsession with self-improvement through a focus on our individual insecurities. I want to be clear—food is there to be enjoyed, first and foremost. Food can make you strong and healthy but you first must accept yourself for who you are. Focus on your strengths, not your weaknesses. It is most important to nourish our bodies for what they are and not to punish them for what they're not. Eating a

certain way shouldn't consume our every waking hour though, either. There was a time in my life when I was extremely focused on avoiding certain food groups and 'clean' eating and it absorbed too much of my energy. It didn't make me happy. I believe it is good to be mindful about what we eat but not to be too stressed about it.

The food in this book is the type of food I cook for my family and friends. They're chef-free recipes, tested by my family and friends in the type of kitchens you all have at home. They're simple and tasty and they are meals you can enjoy every night of the week, knowing that you are looking after your body.

PANTRY STAPLES

To give you a head start, here is a list of what you would find in my kitchen. I'm a frugal girl so I rarely use an ingredient only once—you will see all these ingredients dotted throughout the entire book.

From the refrigerator
Anchovies
Butter
Capers
Cheese: Parmesan, Fresh Ricotta (p. 182), Gruyère, mascarpone, feta, goat's, labneh (p. 183)
Cream: sour, thickened and pure
Mustard: Dijon and whole grain—look for wheat and sugar free
Eggs: free range
Frozen edamame pods
Harissa Paste: homemade (p. 190)
Mayonnaise: homemade (p. 178)
Milk: full cream dairy and Fresh Cashew Milk (p. 180)
Miso: unpasteurized brown rice and white
Natural Greek yogurt: full fat and unsweetened
Pickled jalapeño (no added sugar)

On the shelf
Buckwheat (raw and toasted)
Canned lentils, butter beans, chickpeas, four bean mix, cannellini
Chicken Broth: homemade (p. 187)
Chocolate (dark 70 per cent cacao, milk and white)
Coconut: shredded, desiccated, flaked, coconut milk, coconut cream, coconut chips
Cornflour (cornstarch)
Curry Powder: homemade (p. 191)
Dried fruit: dates, figs, sultanas, semi-dried tomatoes, cranberries
Dried split red lentils

Dry sherry

Fish sauce (sugar and wheat free)

Gluten free rolled oats

Honey

Lemongrass: To prepare, peel the tough, fibrous layers back and discard until you're left with the white centre.

Millet

Mushrooms, dried shiitake

Noodles: rice noodles, buckwheat soba, brown rice and vermicelli

Nut butter: almond and peanut

Nuts and seeds; almonds (whole, slivered, flaked and ground), cashews, macadamia, pistachios, pecans, pine nuts, walnuts, wild rice, chia, pumpkin, sesame, sunflower, poppyseed

Oils: olive, extra virgin olive, rice bran, coconut

Pomegranate molasses

Pure maple syrup

Quinoa: white, red, black and tricolor

Rice: brown, brown basmati, black (forbidden), red

Sea salt flakes

Sesame oil (toasted and untoasted)

Shrimp paste

Spices: cumin (seeds and ground), coriander (seeds and ground), cinnamon (ground and quills), paprika (smoked and sweet), peppercorns (black, white, Sichuan), chili (ground chili, cayenne, chipotle flakes, chili flakes, whole dried chili), fennel seeds, turmeric, sumac, five spice, garam masala, chipotle chili, mixed spice, star anise, yellow mustard seeds, allspice, saffron, nutmeg, cardamom (ground and pods), ground ginger

Tahini

Tamari

Tamarind purée

Tandoori Spice Mix (homemade, p. 189)

Tomato paste

Tomatoes (tinned diced and tomato paste)

Vanilla (pure extract and pods)

Vinegars: apple cider, white wine, red wine, rice wine (gluten free), sherry, balsamic, white balsamic

In the garden

Basics: lemons, limes, garlic, ginger, turmeric

Herbs: lemongrass, basil, mint, coriander (cilantro), tarragon, flat leaf parsley, dill, thyme, chives, oregano, Kaffir lime leaves

Shallots: Asian, eschallots (French shallots)

Spring onions (scallions)

A FEW KITCHEN NOTES

Dairy—I eat full fat dairy however you can easily use low-fat varieties but just be mindful of the sugar content. When selecting yogurt, if you are gluten intolerant, just check the ingredient label to make sure there are no added flours. For yogurt, there should only really be milk present.

Fats—I emphasise using old-fashioned fats (olive oil, sesame, coconut, extra virgin olive oil and butter) in my cooking and avoid vegetable and processed oils.

Sea salt—I prefer to use sea salt when I cook. Please note that the measurements given are not interchangeable with regular table salt. If you are using fine, table salt, only half the amount is required.

Soaking grains—soaking all your grains is a wonderful habit (if you have the time). This ancient technique, which is also known as culturing, helps to release highly beneficial nutrients from the grain and also breaks down the anti-nutrients and hard-to-digest components of the grain and this process allows your body to absorb them better. For the purposes of this book, soaking also shortens the cooking time. The measurements and times I have included here are for grains that have not been soaked so please adjust the times and quantities accordingly. Also, toasting your grains before cooking will enrich the flavor so if you get the chance, go for it.

Tempeh—is made from whole, fermented soybeans. It has a similar texture and flavor to tofu but is nutritionally superior as it is higher in fibre and a great source of iron. (See tofu below)

Tahini—there are two varieties of this sesame seed paste available; hulled tahini has the outer husk removed while unhulled includes the husk and while it is the least refined, it can be slightly bitter.

Tamari—is similar to soy sauce but is either wheat free or has minimal wheat. Look for gluten free if you are gluten intolerant or feel free to substitute with soy sauce if you're not.

Tofu—the world of nutrition is divided as to whether tofu is a health food; whether it is good for us or not. The dilemma is mostly about genetically modified tofu. Currently, most of the world's soybeans are grown in the US, and a very large proportion is genetically modified. If you want to eat tofu, you may consider opting for non-GMO, organic tofu brands. I don't eat tofu on a daily basis. (See Tempeh above.)

Read the labels—I'm one of those people standing in the supermarket aisle reading the ingredient list. I haven't always been like this but experience has taught me that not all products are created equal. Companies often sneak sugar and extra salt into staples such as mustard, peanut butter and even coconut milk.

Store-bought—if you don't have the energy to make ricotta, harissa, labneh, broth or anything else I've included (we are all human, don't worry), try to invest in the best quality ingredients you can afford. As an example, buy good quality stock or broth rather than powdered versions which can be full of sugar and preservatives. If you use powdered stock, try to buy one with as few additives as you can or, better than powdered stock, use water.

Microplane—this is one kitchen tool I couldn't live without. It is a hand-held metal grater that you can use to zest lemons (or any citrus fruit) and finely grate garlic, ginger and Parmesan. Whenever a recipe calls for 'finely grated', I suggest a Microplane (or equivalent zester/grater) is the way to go.

DIETARY GUIDELINES

For each recipe, I have included a breakdown of the following dietary requirements.

- Vegan
- Vegetarian—including eggs and dairy (lacto-ovo vegetarian)
- Sugar Free
- Refined Sugar Free—included when using fruit (fresh or dried), maple syrup, agave nectar or honey
- Dairy Free
- Paleo Friendly—including small amounts of tamari and sesame seeds.
- Gluten Free—based on the use of homemade chicken broth or vegetable broth (store-bought versions often contain wheat), flour free Dijon mustard, gluten free yogurt (some brands in US contain flour), wheat free wasabi, 100 per cent fish sauce and gluten free brown rice miso in recipes. Any alternative suggestions in brackets may not be gluten free.

Breakfast *Love*

I can't skip breakfast, ever. Regardless of how early I wake up or whether I'm running around for meetings, I always make sure I prepare breakfast at home. I lean towards protein-rich options that will stop mid-morning hunger pangs and get me through to lunch. I'm currently in a love affair with eggs, specifically Mexican Scrambled Eggs (p. 20). It's a scrambled pillow of creamy eggs studded with spicy jalapeño, with a fresh lift from a good handful of coriander (cilantro) and chopped tomatoes. I also find myself craving the Thyme and Garlic Magic Mushrooms with Poached Eggs and Chimichurri (p. 19) and not just for breakfast, it doubles as an easy dinner. The Shakshuka Bolognese (p. 29), a shameless fusion of Middle Eastern and Italian flavors, is an undeniable luxury for when you have a little more time, however the Soaked Pineapple and Coconut Pina Colada Oats (p. 24) is ideal for bulk breakfasts and is great for an easy, on-the-go option.

THYME AND GARLIC MAGIC MUSHROOMS
WITH POACHED EGGS AND CHIMICHURRI

These truly are magic mushrooms—and they're legal. Sautéing the mushrooms initially without oil or butter lures out the mushies' water content, which allows them to crisp up when tossed with the butter, garlic and thyme. Topped with a gooey poached egg and scattered with generous dollops of fresh, chili-spiked chimichurri (I could honestly put chimichurri on everything), this dish will leave you nourished and satisfied.

INGREDIENTS

Thyme and garlic mushrooms
600 g (1 lb 5 oz) mixed mushrooms (such as button, oyster, king trumpet), wiped clean, stems removed and halved lengthways
pinch of sea salt
2 tablespoons extra virgin olive oil
2 tablespoons unsalted butter
4 garlic cloves, finely chopped
4 sprigs thyme, roughly chopped

Poached eggs
1 teaspoon apple cider vinegar
4–8 free range eggs, room temperature
100 g (3½ oz) Chimichurri (p. 179)
Labneh (p. 183)

METHOD

- Place mushrooms and a generous pinch of sea salt in a large, dry (do not add butter or oil) frying pan and heat to a medium-high temperature. Cook, stirring occasionally, until the mushrooms release most of their liquid, about 10 minutes. Add oil, butter, garlic and thyme and continue to cook until golden brown all over, about 3 minutes more.
- To poach eggs, bring a medium saucepan of water to a simmer. Add vinegar and then carefully crack 1 egg into the water. Make sure the water does not boil. Gently simmer for 3–4 minutes or until whites have firmed. Remove egg with a slotted spoon and drain on absorbent paper. Repeat process with remaining eggs. If you'd like to serve 2 eggs per person, poach 8 eggs.
- Place mushrooms in the bottom of the bowl, top with 1–2 poached eggs and scatter with spoonfuls of chimichurri and labneh. If you're not gluten intolerant, sourdough toast would make a great side.

Note: When poaching, more so than any other cooking method, it's crucial to have fresh eggs. The easiest way to tell whether an egg is fresh is to submerge it in cold water. It should sink to the bottom and stay there. If it floats to the top, the egg is no longer fresh. To make this paleo, omit the labneh.

MEXICAN SCRAMBLED EGGS WITH AVOCADO

While this dish does tend to have a certain *je ne sais quoi* after a night of too many wines, please don't wait for that as the impetus to try it. I have been known to toss through sautéed kale for an extra boost of greens. If you have any leftover Roasted Mixed Potatoes (p. 157) in the refrigerator, throw them in the pan with the eggs and you'll be ready for anything—hangover or no hangover. Soda water is my secret ingredient for creating fluffy, cloud-like scrambled eggs.

INGREDIENTS

6–8 free range eggs

sea salt and freshly ground black pepper

3 tablespoons soda water or sparkling mineral water

1 tablespoon extra virgin olive oil

½ small brown onion, peeled and finely diced

1 garlic clove, finely chopped

1–2 jalapeño chilies or green chili, deseeded and finely chopped

1 plum tomato, cored, deseeded, and finely diced

small handful coriander (cilantro), roughly chopped

1 avocado, peeled, de-stoned and thinly sliced

METHOD

- Crack the eggs into a bowl. Add a pinch of salt and pepper and use a fork or whisk to gently beat. Add soda water and stir to combine. Set aside.
- Heat the oil to a medium temperature in a large, non-stick frying pan. Add the onion and cook until lightly golden. Stir through the garlic, chilies and tomato and cook for 1–2 minutes.
- Add eggs and stir slowly with a wooden spoon until the eggs look silky, slightly runny and slightly underdone and then remove from the heat.
- Stir through coriander, divide between bowls and add the sliced avocado on the side.

CINNAMON CHIA OATS WITH BANANA CHUNKS AND COCONUT CHIPS

While the oats cook, the banana chunks soften into sweet, soft and forgiving mouthfuls. The chia seeds add texture and a protein boost—if you like the texture of chia, feel free to add a little more, as I do. Chia seeds are the second highest plant-based source of omega-3 fatty acids and one of the most easily digestible plant proteins.

INGREDIENTS

120 g (4 oz) gluten free rolled oats
375 ml (12 fl oz) Fresh Cashew Milk (p. 180) or milk of choice
250 ml (8 fl oz) water
2 tablespoons chia seeds
2 ripe firm bananas, roughly chopped
pinch of sea salt
1 teaspoon ground cinnamon
1 teaspoon vanilla extract
2 tablespoons coconut chips (or shredded coconut)

METHOD

- In a medium saucepan, combine oats, cashew milk, water, chia seeds, banana and a pinch of salt.
- Bring to the boil and then simmer over medium low heat, stirring often, until the liquid has been absorbed and the oats become thick and creamy, about 10 minutes.
- Remove from the heat and stir in cinnamon and vanilla.
- Divide the chia oats between bowls and top with coconut chips.

CARROT CAKE SPICED BUCKWHEAT PORRIDGE

Despite its name, buckwheat contains no wheat and isn't actually a grain at all—it's the seed of a plant related to rhubarb. For those mornings when oats seem a bit dense and heavy, this buckwheat porridge has a lighter, cleaner texture, with flecks of sweet carrots, tart apple and chewy coconut that really does remind one of carrot cake.

INGREDIENTS

100 g (3½ oz) raw buckwheat, washed and drained

500 ml (16 fl oz) Fresh Cashew Milk (p. 180) or milk of choice

1 Pink Lady apple (or other variety), coarsely grated

1 carrot, peeled and grated

40 g (1½ oz) shredded coconut

1 teaspoon vanilla extract

1 teaspoon ground cinnamon

½ teaspoon mixed spice

pinch of sea salt

3–4 tablespoons sultanas, roughly chopped

2 tablespoons walnuts or pecans, roughly chopped

pure maple syrup (if vegan) or honey, to drizzle

1 persimmon (optional), thinly sliced

METHOD

- Place buckwheat, cashew milk, apple, carrot, coconut, vanilla, cinnamon, mixed spice, salt and sultanas together in a medium saucepan. Over a gentle heat, stir regularly until buckwheat is cooked and the mixture has thickened, about 30 minutes.
- Divide porridge between 4 bowls. Serve with persimmon slices, scatter with extra grated carrot, coconut, nuts and drizzle with honey or maple syrup, if desired.

SOAKED PINEAPPLE
AND COCONUT PINA COLADA OATS

Soaking any grain overnight makes it easier for the body to digest and absorb the nutrients. This recipe shakes up the usual bircher muesli (as it's known in Australia) combination, with a tropical, pina colada vibe, sans white rum.

INGREDIENTS

100 g (3½ oz) gluten free rolled oats

400 ml (14 fl oz) coconut milk or Fresh Cashew Milk (p. 180)

125 g (4½ oz) coconut yogurt (for dairy free) or Greek yogurt

40 g (1½ oz) shredded or desiccated coconut

1 teaspoon vanilla extract

½ teaspoon turmeric

½ teaspoon ground cinnamon

¼ teaspoon sea salt

200 g (7 oz) pineapple, peeled, tough inner core removed and flesh cut into 1 cm (½ in) pieces

METHOD

- The night before, mix the oats, coconut milk, yogurt, coconut, vanilla, turmeric, cinnamon, salt and pineapple together in a bowl. Cover and soak overnight.
- In the morning, divide the mixture between 4 bowls and top with additional pineapple and yogurt, if desired.

BACON AND EGG BREAKFAST RAMEN

If you're gluten free, ramen is a dish that you usually have to do without, which I think is simply unfair and the reason I decided to create this bowl. A traditional ramen broth takes days to prepare but for anybody who wants to make ramen quickly, here's an excellent shortcut recipe. I use 100 per cent brown rice ramen noodles however buckwheat soba are perfect too.

INGREDIENTS

Miso broth
1 L (2 pt) Chicken Broth (p. 187) or store-bought stock
2 teaspoons brown rice or white (shiro) miso paste
½ teaspoon ginger, finely grated
1 teaspoon sesame oil
1 tablespoon tamari (or light soy sauce)

Toppings
4 large free range eggs
250 g (9 oz) dried brown rice ramen or soba (100 per cent buckwheat) noodles
4 bacon rashers, rindless (optional)
2 teaspoons chili flakes or any chili paste (optional)
2 spring onions (scallions), finely sliced

METHOD

- Pour chicken broth into a medium saucepan and bring to a simmer. Add miso and whisk to combine. Stir through ginger, sesame oil and tamari; taste and add more tamari, if necessary. (The broth should be well seasoned). Cover and, over a gentle simmer, cook for atleast 10 minutes or until ready to serve.
- Meanwhile, place water and a generous pinch of sea salt in a large saucepan and bring to the boil. Reduce heat to a simmer, gently submerge eggs and cook for exactly 6 minutes. Drain and run under cold water (if you prefer hard-boiled eggs, cook for 7–8 minutes). Once cool enough to handle, remove shell and slice in half lengthways.
- Cook the noodles according to packet instructions and drain well.
- To cook the bacon, heat a non-stick frying pan over a medium-high temperature. Add bacon and cook, turning once, until crisp, about 3–4 minutes. Drain on absorbent paper.
- When ready to eat, divide noodles between bowls and then ladle piping hot miso broth over each serving. Top with egg, crispy bacon rashers, chili and spring onions.

Note: Bacon is not a wholefood ingredient I recommend on a daily basis, which is why I have included this as an optional ingredient. For any clean eating purists, just top with an egg, but for a little weekend indulgence, a slice of bacon works a treat.

CHUNKY STICKY DATE PUDDING GRANOLA
WITH BANANA NICE CREAM

I feel as though I harp on about the superiority of homemade granola so I won't waste my breath here, except to say that this is my favorite combination yet. I recently took a batch of this to a friend's beach house and the person on 'nibbles duty' was running late—instead, we feasted on handfuls of this granola and nobody seemed too interested in the dips platter when it arrived. Banana nice cream is my secret kitchen trick—when frozen banana is blended, it makes creamy and thick ice-cream (due to its high pectin content).

INGREDIENTS

Banana nice cream
4 ripe bananas, peeled and roughly
    chopped

Granola
200 g (7 oz) gluten free rolled oats
75 g (2¾ oz) whole raw cashews
75 g (2¾ oz) raw macadamias, roughly
    chopped
120 g (4 oz) fresh (or dried) dates,
    pitted and roughly chopped
40 g (1½ oz) shredded coconut
1 teaspoon ground cinnamon
1 teaspoon ground mixed spice
pinch of sea salt
3–4 tablespoons pure maple syrup
100 ml (3½ fl oz) coconut (or olive) oil
1 teaspoon vanilla extract

Toppings
1 punnet fresh blueberries
1 punnet of strawberries, halved
2 passionfruit, pulp scooped out
2 kiwifruit, peeled and sliced
1 mandarin, peeled into segments
Edible flowers (optional)

METHOD

- Begin this recipe the day before by placing the peeled bananas into a container or zip lock bag to freeze overnight.
- Preheat oven to 160°C (320°F) and line a tray with baking (parchment) paper.
- In a large bowl combine all the dry ingredients; oats, cashews, macadamias, dates, coconut, cinnamon, mixed spice and salt.
- Heat maple syrup and coconut oil in a small saucepan over a gentle temperature. Once the coconut oil has melted, add vanilla and pour over the dry ingredients. Toss to combine.
- Spread mixture evenly onto the lined tray, and bake for 30 minutes, stirring once about halfway through. Remove from the oven and leave to cool completely—do not stir at this stage.
- When ready to eat, make the banana nice cream. Blend frozen bananas with a high-powered stick blender or food processor and purée until smooth, stopping occasionally to scrape down the sides.
- Divide nice cream between bowls and scatter with granola, fresh fruit and edible flowers (if using).

Note: This makes about 600 g (1 lb 5 oz) of granola. A quick hint on the dates: if you're using fresh dates, they're easier to chop cold, so pop them in the refrigerator or freezer for 15 minutes before chopping.

CHIA ANZAC COOKIES

Let me justify why this recipe is in a bowl food cookbook—because these cookies have been known, and I'm not naming names, to be devoured by the bowlful and, before you scoff (pun intended), I challenge you to tell me why I can't eat them by the bowlful. These virtuous little bites are chock-full of the good stuff; rolled oats, coconut, almonds, chia seeds and a dash of honey.

INGREDIENTS

180 g (6¼ oz) gluten free rolled oats
50 g (1¾ oz) desiccated or flaked
    coconut
50 g (1¾ oz) flaked (or blanched
    whole) almonds
3 tablespoons macadamia oil (or any
    nut, coconut or olive oil)
2 tablespoons honey (or maple syrup
    for vegan option)
1 teaspoon vanilla extract
1 tablespoon chia seeds
¼ teaspoon ground cinnamon
3 tablespoons hot water

METHOD

- Preheat oven to 150°C (300°F).
- Place oats, coconut and almonds in a food processor and process until the nuts break down. Add the oil, honey, vanilla, chia seeds, cinnamon and water and process again until it forms a dough-like consistency. If the mixture is too crumbly, add a little more water.
- Shape into 25 small cookies and place on a tray lined with baking (parchment) paper. Flatten down with your hand or a spatula, ensuring there's enough room around each cookie. Bake for 20–30 minutes or until lightly golden.

Note: Store in an airtight container for 5 days.

SHAKSHUKA BOLOGNESE

Much to the horror of any shakshuka purists, in this recipe I have sacrificed authenticity and added beef mince, which, I must say, has been a bit of a hit in our household. For a stress-free brunch, start this the night before and then in the morning, simply crack in the eggs and serve.

INGREDIENTS

1 tablespoon extra virgin olive oil

3 garlic cloves, finely chopped

½ onion, peeled and finely diced

500 g (1 lb 2 oz) beef mince

1 tablespoon Harissa Paste (p. 190) or store-bought paste

½ teaspoon ground cumin

1 tablespoon tomato paste

1 x 400 g (14 oz) tin diced tomatoes

4 free range eggs

METHOD

- Heat the olive oil in a large frying pan to a medium temperature. Add the garlic and onion and cook until softened, about 3 minutes. Add the beef and cook, stirring to break up any lumps, for 5 minutes or until browned.
- Stir through the harissa, cumin, tomato paste and tinned tomatoes. Reduce heat and, stirring occasionally, simmer for 10–15 minutes or until you have a thick sauce. At this point, taste the shakshuka and, if you prefer more spice, add more harissa.
- Make 4 small indents around the tomato mixture and gently crack an egg into each indent. Cover with a frying pan lid, reduce heat to low and cook for 4–6 minutes or until egg white is cooked and yolk is still runny (if you prefer your egg yolks hard, cook for a further 2 minutes).
- Place frying pan in the middle of the table and let everyone help themselves.

Note: Shakshuka is a traditional, tomato-based egg dish that originated in North Africa. A sprinkling of feta, when serving, makes a lovely addition.

Whet the *Appetite*

I make no apology for not eating all meals with cutlery. There's something comforting and convivial about ditching the fork and getting your fingers dirty; a sort of fuss-free meal. Or perhaps it's just plain laziness and my way of minimising washing up. Either way, I think bowls overflowing with finger food make eating a social, friendly affair. To me, sharing a bowl of food is quite intimate. Whether you're entertaining or if it's just a dinner date for two, passing around bowls of food—lingering over each mouthful, nibbling a little of this or sharing some of that—what a pleasurable way to enjoy a meal.

I really do encourage you to try the Salmon San Choy Bao (p. 36). It's the sort of dish that I crave, a little too regularly. Munching on a bowl of Sticky Tamarind, Sesame and Lime Chicken Wings (p. 42) is perfect for family affairs and for those cold, rainy days when you can't leave the couch. If you're eager to impress, the Parmesan, Ricotta and Gruyère Sweet Potato Arancini Balls with Basil Mayonnaise (p. 35) will do just that, and the Marinated Mushrooms with Garlic, Chili and White Balsamic Vinegar (p. 39) is perfect to have on hand for a simple pre-dinner nibble or to construct an ad hoc salad bowl.

CURRIED PUMPKIN SOUP
WITH TANDOORI CHICKPEAS

Everyone is looking for creative ways to use up the humble ol' pumpkin and I've got to say, this is simple and delicious. The tandoori chickpeas are special just by themselves so whip up a double batch to use as a pre-dinner nibble the next day. Rather than tossing the pumpkin skin away, cut it into small pieces and roast with the tandoori chickpeas (the skin crisps up into the most delicious crunchy pieces).

INGREDIENTS

Tandoori chickpeas

1 x 400 g (14 oz) tin chickpeas, drained and rinsed

1 tablespoon Tandoori Spice Mix (p. 189) or store-bought tandoori paste

1 tablespoon extra virgin olive oil

Curried pumpkin soup

2 tablespoons extra virgin olive oil

1 large red onion, finely diced

2 garlic cloves, finely chopped

1 teaspoon ginger, finely grated

1 kg (2 lb 3 oz) butternut pumpkin (or any pumpkin or squash of choice), peeled and cut into even size pieces

2 tablespoons Curry Powder (p. 191) or store-bought

1 teaspoon cinnamon

400 ml (14 fl oz) coconut milk

500 ml (16 fl oz) Vegetable Broth (p. 188) or any broth/stock of choice

2 tablespoons coriander (cilantro), roughly chopped

METHOD

- Preheat oven to 200°C (400°F).
- Using absorbent paper or a clean kitchen towel, pat chickpeas dry and place in a small bowl with tandoori spice mix and oil. (If using store-bought tandoori paste, omit oil). Toss to coat the chickpeas, then spread evenly in a single layer onto a tray lined with baking (parchment) paper. Transfer to the oven and roast until golden, tossing occasionally, about 20–25 minutes. Turn off the oven and leave the door slightly open. Allow the chickpeas to cool completely on the tray (in the oven) to crisp up.
- Meanwhile, heat the oil in a large saucepan to a medium temperature. Add onion, garlic and ginger. Stirring regularly, cook until softened and lightly golden, about 2 minutes. Add pumpkin, curry powder and cinnamon and stir to coat before adding coconut milk and broth. Reduce heat to a low temperature, cover and simmer for 25–30 minutes or until the pumpkin is tender when pierced with a fork.
- Purée the soup using a high-powered stick blender or food processor. Season to taste. Divide the soup between bowls, drizzle with a little extra coconut milk (optional) and scatter with tandoori chickpeas and coriander.

Note: Store leftover soup covered in the refrigerator for 3–4 days, or in the freezer for up to 1 month. Store chickpeas separately in an airtight container at room temperature for up to 2 days. Skip the tandoori chickpeas to make this dish paleo.

VIRTUOUS GREEN SOUP WITH MINTED CRÈME FRAÎCHE

Glancing at the ingredients, this is indeed a virtuous medley of ingredients but let me assure you, you won't be able to taste the restraint in this soup. Cauliflower contains pectin (yes, the same thing that sets your jam), which is wonderful for using in a soup as the cauliflower becomes naturally creamy and thick when cooked. The key ingredient is homemade broth (or, at the very least, good quality store-bought stock) to give it a rich depth of flavor.

INGREDIENTS

2 tablespoons extra virgin olive oil

1 onion, finely chopped

6 garlic cloves, roughly chopped

1 L (2 pt) Chicken Broth (p. 187) or Vegetable Broth (for vegetarian, p. 188)

½ large cauliflower (about 600 g / 1 lb 5 oz), trimmed and broken into small florets

400 g (14 oz) (about 1 bunch) English spinach, washed and roughly chopped

3 tablespoons crème fraîche

1 tablespoon fresh mint, finely chopped

sea salt and freshly ground black pepper

METHOD

- Heat the oil in a large saucepan to a medium-high temperature. Add onion and garlic and stir occasionally until softened, about 3–4 minutes. Stir through chicken broth and cauliflower and bring to the boil. Reduce heat, cover with a lid and simmer until cauliflower is tender, about 15 minutes. Add spinach, cover again and simmer until the spinach is just cooked, about 2–3 minutes.
- Using a high-powered stick blender or food processor, purée the soup until creamy and smooth. Taste and adjust seasoning, as required.
- Place crème fraîche and mint in a small bowl and stir to combine. Season to taste.
- To serve, ladle soup into bowls and serve hot with a dollop of minted crème fraîche.

PARMESAN, RICOTTA AND GRUYÈRE SWEET POTATO ARANCINI BALLS WITH BASIL MAYONNAISE

I'm going to say it: these are the best arancini balls I've ever eaten—better than the classic, deep-fried ones I've eaten at many an Italian restaurant. I don't feel boastful in saying this as the goodness lies in the simple combination of ingredients; a mixture of gooey cheese, rolled up with the pillowy-lightness and earthiness of steamed sweet potato and thyme and then roasted to a crisp. *Delizioso*.

INGREDIENTS

100 g (3½ oz) brown rice (or same amount cooked brown rice)

250 ml (8 fl oz) water

300 g (10½ oz) sweet potato, peeled and chopped into even rounds

100 g (3½ oz) Fresh Ricotta (p. 182) or store-bought

100 g (3½ oz) Parmesan cheese, grated

25 g (1 oz) Gruyère cheese

1 free range egg, lightly beaten

1 teaspoon sea salt

½ teaspoon freshly ground black pepper

2 teaspoons fresh thyme, finely chopped

Basil mayonnaise

½ bunch basil, finely chopped

2 teaspoons lemon juice

100 g (3½ oz) Whole Egg Mayonnaise (p. 178) or store-bought

METHOD

- Preheat oven to 200°C (400°F) and line a roasting tray with baking (parchment) paper.
- Start by steaming your brown rice. Wash rice under cold running water and drain. Place rice, water and a pinch of salt in a saucepan and bring to the boil. Reduce heat to a low temperature, cover and simmer until rice is just tender and the water has evaporated, about 30–35 minutes. Set aside and allow to cool to room temperature.
- Over a saucepan of simmering water, steam sweet potato until soft, about 18–20 minutes. Once cooked, remove from the heat and place in a bowl.
- Using a potato masher or the back of a fork, mash sweet potato. Add cooled rice, ricotta, Parmesan, Gruyère, egg, salt, pepper and thyme and stir to combine.
- Roll the mixture into 20 x 4 cm (1½ in) balls. Place on the prepared tray and cook in the oven for 20 minutes or until golden on the outside.
- Meanwhile, prepare the basil mayonnaise by combining basil, lemon juice and mayonnaise in a bowl.
- Serve hot arancini balls with basil mayonnaise.

Note: The arancini balls can be done ahead of time and simply roasted when your guests arrive. To make this vegetarian, omit the Parmesan and leave the anchovies out of the mayonnaise.

SALMON SAN CHOY BAO

This dish came to fruition when I forgot to buy mince to make san choy bao but happened to have a few salmon fillets in the refrigerator—hello, salmon san choy bao. I wasn't sure if it was a winning dish until I served it to family and friends. The first night I cooked it, everyone asked for the recipe. I wish I could say all my kitchen mistakes worked out so successfully.

INGREDIENTS

6–8 dried shiitake mushrooms, soaked in hot water for 20 minutes and roughly chopped

400 g (14 oz) salmon (or ocean trout) fillet, skinless and pin-boned

1 free range egg white

2 tablespoons coconut oil or rice bran oil

1 small brown onion, finely diced

3 garlic cloves, finely chopped

1 teaspoon fresh ginger, finely grated

2 tablespoons tamari (or light soy sauce)

1 tablespoon dry sherry (or Shaoxing rice wine if you can tolerate gluten)

1 teaspoon sesame oil

100 g (3½ oz) water chestnut slices, roughly chopped

100 g (3½ oz) bamboo shoots, roughly chopped

8 baby cos lettuce cups or ½ head iceberg lettuce, separated

3 spring onions (scallions), thinly sliced

1 long red chili, deseeded and thinly sliced lengthways

METHOD

- Place dried mushrooms in a small heatproof bowl. Cover with boiling water and soak for 20–30 minutes or until softened.
- Using a slotted spoon, remove mushrooms, reserving 2 tablespoons of the soaking liquid. Finely chop mushrooms.
- Cut the salmon into 2 cm (¾ in) cubes and place in a bowl. Add egg white and toss to coat.
- Heat 1 tablespoon of oil in a wok to a high temperature. Add the onion, garlic, ginger and chopped mushrooms and stir-fry until lightly golden, about 3 minutes. Remove from the wok and set aside.
- Heat the remaining oil in the wok and fry the salmon pieces until golden on all sides. Add the tamari, sherry and sesame oil and toss to coat the salmon. Return the mushroom and onion mix to the wok. Add water chestnuts, bamboo shoots and reserved mushroom liquid and toss to combine.
- To serve, fill the lettuce cups with salmon and scatter with spring onions and chili.

CRAB, CHILI AND AVOCADO LETTUCE BOATS

Fresh, crunchy lettuce boats filled with a jumble of sweet-picked crab and avocado chunks. This dish reminds me of an Australian summer; all that's missing is a glass of crisp, cold white wine, a clear starry night and dear friends on the beach. If you can't find crab, you can substitute with cooked prawns (shrimp), peeled, deveined and roughly chopped.

INGREDIENTS

220 g (7¾ oz) cooked white crab meat (preferably blue swimmer)
3 spring onions (scallions), finely sliced
1 ripe avocado, diced
1 long red chili, deseed and finely chopped
½ bunch coriander (cilantro), leaves picked and chopped
2 tablespoons lemon juice
1½ tablespoons sherry vinegar (or red wine vinegar)
1 tablespoon extra virgin olive oil
sea salt and freshly ground black pepper
Baby Gem lettuce heads, washed and leaves separated
pinch of paprika (optional)

METHOD

- Place crab, spring onions, avocado, chili and coriander in a bowl. Combine lemon juice, sherry vinegar and extra virgin olive oil in a small jug. Pour dressing over crab mixture and toss to combine. Season to taste.
- Divide crab between lettuce cups and sprinkle with paprika.

MARINATED MUSHROOMS
WITH GARLIC, CHILI AND WHITE BALSAMIC VINEGAR

I use balsamic vinegar with caution as it can overtake a dish but, I'll glug white balsamic vinegar over anything and everything. Unlike its ostentatious sibling, white balsamic vinegar will happily share the limelight with other ingredients, adding a delicate flavor with just a hint of sweetness. These marinated mushrooms are best made ahead of time and will last up to 7 days in the refrigerator.

INGREDIENTS

250 g (9 oz) button mushrooms, brushed and halved

1 long red chili, deseeded, finely chopped

2 garlic cloves, finely chopped

2 spring onions (scallions), finely sliced

2 tablespoons flat leaf parsley, roughly chopped

100 ml (3½ fl oz) extra virgin olive oil

100 ml (3½ fl oz) white balsamic vinegar

sea salt and freshly ground white pepper

Seedy Superfood Crackers (p. 45), to serve

METHOD

- Combine all ingredients in a bowl and toss to combine. Season to taste with salt and pepper.
- Place in the refrigerator and allow to marinate at least overnight, stirring occasionally, or for up to 7 days. Serve with seedy superfood crackers.

LOADED BLACK BEAN NACHOS WITH SWEET POTATO, FETA AND JALAPEÑO GUACAMOLE

This dish embodies everything that I love about bowl food—contrasting textures and a tangle of delicious little mouthfuls to create comfort food at its best. I've substituted sweet potato with potato and made it without black beans and switched the beef mince for turkey mince—as you can see, the variations are limitless.

INGREDIENTS

2 sweet potatoes
3 tablespoons coconut oil, melted
large pinch of sea salt
3 tablespoons feta, goat's cheese or sour cream
handful of heirloom or cherry tomatoes, halved
2 tablespoons fresh micro coriander (cilantro)
1 lime, quartered

Spicy Mexican beef
1 tablespoon olive or coconut oil
½ large red onion, finely diced
½ red capsicum (bell pepper), finely diced
2 garlic cloves, finely chopped
500 g (1 lb 2 oz) beef mince
½ teaspoon ground chili
1 teaspoon smoked paprika
2 teaspoons ground cumin
1 teaspoon ground coriander
1 tablespoon tomato paste
1 x 400 g (14 oz) tin diced tomatoes
1 x 400 g (14 oz) tin black beans, rinsed and drained
sea salt and freshly ground black pepper

Jalapeño guacamole
2 medium ripe avocados
1 garlic clove, finely grated
2 tomatoes, deseeded and diced
1 jalapeño or long red chili, seeds removed, chopped
1 tablespoons fresh lime juice
½ teaspoon ground cumin

METHOD

- Preheat oven to 200°C (400°F).
- Peel and slice the sweet potato lengthways using a mandolin into very thin slices.
- Place sweet potato in a bowl. Drizzle with melted coconut oil and toss to coat. Spread sweet potato, in a single layer, on lined roasting trays. Bake for 10 minutes, then turn over and return to the oven for a further 8–10 minutes or until the edges are golden. Depending on the sweet potatoes, they may need longer in the oven. Season with salt and allow to cool completely to crisp up.
- To make the spicy Mexican beef, heat the oil in a large frying pan to a medium-high temperature. Add the onion, capsicum and garlic and cook until softened, about 3 minutes. Add the beef and cook, stirring to break up any lumps, for 5 minutes or until browned. Add the spices and tomato paste and cook for 1 minute, then mix in the tomatoes. Reduce the heat to low and simmer for 10–12 minutes. Add drained black beans and season with salt and pepper, to taste.
- To make the jalapeño guacamole, scoop out the avocado flesh and place in a large bowl. Add all the remaining ingredients and, using the back of a fork, mash to combine. Taste and season.
- To assemble the nachos, divide spicy beef between bowls, top with guacamole and sweet potato chips and scatter with feta, tomatoes and coriander. Serve with lime wedges alongside.

Note: To make this paleo, leave out the black beans and feta.

STICKY TAMARIND, SESAME AND LIME CHICKEN WINGS

Don't be afraid to get messy—these tangy, baked wings promise to please the tastebuds and, for some reason, they're more delicious when eaten with your hands.

INGREDIENTS

4 tablespoons tamarind purée

1 lime, juiced

2 tablespoons gluten free fish sauce

1 tablespoon tamari (or light soy sauce)

1 teaspoon ground cumin

2 garlic cloves, finely chopped

½ teaspoon ginger, finely grated

1 teaspoon sesame oil

2 tablespoons black and white sesame
  seeds, plus extra to serve

1 tablespoon rice bran oil

1 kg (2 lb 3 oz) free range chicken
  wings, rinsed and patted dry

1 lime, cut into wedges, to serve

METHOD

- Preheat oven to 200°C (400°F).
- Combine the tamarind purée, lime juice, fish sauce, tamari, cumin, garlic, ginger, sesame oil, sesame seeds and oil in a bowl then pour into a zip lock bag or container. Add the wings and toss to coat. Place in the refrigerator and leave to marinate for at least several hours or up to 2 days.
- Arrange the wings on a baking tray and cook for 25–30 minutes, turning half way through, or until the wings are nicely browned and caramelized. Alternatively, preheat a barbecue or char-grill to medium-high and grill, turning occasionally, until golden and cooked through, about 8–10 minutes.
- Place in a large bowl, scatter with extra sesame seeds and serve with lime wedges.

SUNDRIED TOMATO SPREAD

I'll admit, on paper this doesn't look like anything special but whipped up into a rich, tomato-red spread, generously lathered on to some seed-studded crackers and you won't stop going back for more. Fresh basil is key so keep this recipe up your sleeve for when your herb garden is in full bloom.

INGREDIENTS

100 g (3½ oz) sundried tomatoes (not in oil)
125 ml (4 fl oz) boiling water
80 ml (2¾ fl oz) extra virgin olive oil
1 tablespoon red wine vinegar
1 garlic clove, roughly chopped
½ bunch basil, roughly chopped
½ teaspoon sea salt
Seedy Superfood Crackers (p. 45).

METHOD

- Place sundried tomatoes in a small bowl and add just enough boiling water to cover, about 125 ml (4 fl oz). Allow to stand for 5–10 minutes or until tomatoes have softened.
- Place sundried tomatoes (including all the boiling water) in a food processor and purée to a paste.
- Add oil, red wine vinegar, garlic, basil and salt and purée until smooth.
- If not serving immediately, cover the surface of the dip with a splash of extra virgin olive oil and cover. Keep refrigerated until ready to eat.
- Serve with seedy superfood crackers.

SEEDY SUPERFOOD CRACKERS

These are certainly a welcome addition to your recipe repertoire—so simple to make and very versatile. They aren't like normal crackers as they are a little more brittle (and sometimes break when scooping up some dip) but I think that's the beauty of them too—they're not dense but light and crunchy.

INGREDIENTS

100 g (3½ oz) almond meal
75 g (2¾ oz) pumpkin seeds (pepitas)
75 g (2¾ oz) sunflower seeds
75 g (2¾ oz) chia seeds
40 g (1½ oz) sesame seeds
200 ml (7 oz) water
2 tablespoons extra virgin olive oil
½ teaspoon sesame oil
1 teaspoon sea salt flakes
½ teaspoon freshly ground black pepper

METHOD

- Preheat oven to 180°C (350°F) and line 2 trays with baking (parchment) paper.
- In a large bowl, stir to combine almond meal, pumpkin seeds, sunflower seeds, chia seeds and sesame seeds. Add water, olive oil and sesame oil and stir to make a wet dough. Set aside for 5 minutes to allow the chia seeds to absorb some of the liquid.
- Once the mixture has thickened, divide into 2 and place on prepared trays. Using a spatula or your hands, spread the dough out as thinly as possible.
- Sprinkle salt and pepper over mixture and bake for 30–35 minutes or until just golden. Remove from oven and allow to cool completely. Break into pieces to serve.
- Store in an airtight container if not eating immediately.

HERBED FETA DIP
WITH FARMERS' MARKET CRUDITÉS

This creamy concoction is studded with fresh chopped herbs and pairs particularly well with the season's bounty—here sweet cherry tomatoes, baby carrots and crisp snap and sugar peas—but let your local farmers' market or green grocer (or, better yet, your own garden) be your guide.

INGREDIENTS

200 g (7 oz) Danish feta
100 g (3½ oz) natural Greek yogurt
2 tablespoons lemon juice
½ bunch fresh flat leaf parsley, finely chopped
¼ bunch fresh mint, finely chopped
2 tablespoons finely chopped fresh dill, plus torn sprigs for serving
sea salt and freshly ground black pepper
1 tablespoon extra virgin olive oil
Seedy Superfood Crackers (p. 45), to serve

Assorted crudités
colorful cherry tomatoes
baby heirloom carrots
red radishes, halved
snap peas
snow peas
baby asparagus

METHOD

- Place feta, yogurt and lemon juice in a food processor. (If you don't have a food processor, you can whisk by hand). Blend until smooth before transferring to a medium bowl. Add parsley, mint and dill and stir to combine. Season to taste.
- For the crudités, work in batches and blanch baby carrots, radishes, snap peas, snow peas and asparagus in a saucepan of salted boiling water until just tender, about 30–60 seconds. Use a slotted spoon to transfer vegetables to an ice-water bath, and let cool completely before removing and patting dry. Halve carrots lengthways before serving. Alternatively, you can serve the vegetables raw.
- To serve, fill a large serving bowl with assorted crudités and seedy superfood crackers. Place dip alongside or in the middle, scattered with extra dill.

From the Sea

Since moving to the UK, I have discovered Elizabeth David, one of Britain's most famous food writers. Her unconventional recipe writing style intertwined the ingredients and method so there's no clear structure, it is more like a story. She believed that recipes are not about giving marching orders to do this and that; they are more like a dance that you (the cook), the ingredients and the recipe writer do together. When cooking, in general, but perhaps more pertinently with seafood, I encourage you to embrace this attitude. Your dance starts at the fishmonger. Buy fresh, sustainable seafood (and not just what is suggested in the recipe) and make changes as you see fit. Worldwide fish stocks are declining and entire marine regions are considered overfished. As a consumer, look for fish varieties that are in season (or just ask your fishmonger). Depending on where you live, there are also various certifications that acknowledge which fish is sustainable.

If you're already a seafood lover, then you won't need me to convince you to try the Green Ceviche (p. 62) or the Lemongrass and Turmeric Seafood Curry (p. 67). For those who are more limited in their access to seafood, the Maple, Green Tea and Lemongrass Salmon Parcels (p. 55) are an easy entertaining option while the Wok Fried Japanese Bubble and Squeak with Prawns and Tamari Mayonnaise (p. 59) may not be much to look at, but that's a compromise I'm willing to make, as it is truly delicious.

INDIAN SPICED ROASTED FISH WITH RED LENTIL DHAL

Spice up your life with these Indian-inspired marinated fish fillets, served with a sweet tomatoey dhal. I'm a hard-core yogurt lover so I have a tendency to be quite generous with my proportions; feel free to halve the amount in the marinade for a more scant 'crust'. This dhal doubles up as a fabulous pre-dinner dip or alongside any Indian or Sri Lankan curry.

INGREDIENTS

4 x 180 g (6¼ oz) ling, cod or any firm white fish fillets, pin-boned and skin removed
1 tablespoon coriander (cilantro), roughly chopped
pappadums, gluten free (optional), to serve
Steamed Coconut and Spring Onion Brown Rice (p. 193), to serve

Yogurt and spice marinade

250 g (9 oz) natural Greek yogurt
½ teaspoon lime zest
2 tablespoons lime juice
3 teaspoons yellow mustard seeds
1 teaspoon garam masala
1 teaspoon sea salt
¼ teaspoon chili powder (optional)

Dhal

200 g (7 oz) dried split red lentils
1 tablespoon extra virgin olive oil
1 small brown onion, peeled and finely diced
3 garlic cloves, finely chopped
1 teaspoon ground cumin
1 teaspoon fresh or ground turmeric
1 teaspoon garam masala
500 ml (16 fl oz) Chicken Broth (p. 187) or any stock/ broth of choice
200 g (7 oz) diced tomato (tinned or fresh)
1 teaspoon sea salt

METHOD

- Preheat oven to 200°C (400°F).
- To make the marinade, combine yogurt, lime zest, juice, mustard seeds, garam masala, salt and chili (if using) in a bowl.
- Place fish in a shallow baking tray. Pour over the marinade and, using your hands, rub to coat.
- While the fish is marinating, make the dhal. Place lentils in a bowl, wash a few times with cold water and drain completely. Heat the oil in a saucepan to a medium-high temperature. Add onion and garlic and sauté until softened and lightly golden, about 2 minutes. Add drained lentils, cumin, turmeric, garam masala, broth and tomato. Reduce heat to a medium-low temperature; cover and cook until the lentils are tender, about 30–35 minutes, stirring occasionally.
- Place fish in the oven and bake until just cooked through, about 15 minutes. Insert a knife or skewer into the flesh to test if the fish is cooked and then touch the knife to your lips. If it's cold, it needs more time but if it's warm, the fish is ready.
- Divide the rice between bowls, top with dhal and roasted fish. Scatter with coriander and serve with pappadums.

Note: If you are gluten intolerant, be sure to check the ingredients of the pappadums.

KAFFIR LIME AND CHILI SEAFOOD SKEWERS WITH MANGO, CUCUMBER AND HERB NOODLE SALAD

Let's talk about kaffir lime leaves. If you're yet to cook with them, you're in for a treat. The moment you rub these outrageously aromatic leaves between your fingers, they release a fragrant lemony-lime scent that infuses these skewers magically. It goes without saying that fresh seafood will make this dish shine.

INGREDIENTS

200 g (7 oz) salmon or ocean trout fillets, skin removed, pin-boned and cut into 3 cm (1¼ in) cubes

200 g (7 oz) white fish fillets, skin removed, pin-boned and cut into 3 cm (1¼ in) cubes

200 g (7 oz) green prawns (shrimp), peeled, deveined, tails intact

100 g (3½ oz) squid tubes, cut into 3 cm (1¼ in) squares

Marinade
3 tablespoons extra virgin olive oil

½ teaspoon dried chili flakes

zest of 2 limes (or lemon)

6 garlic cloves, finely chopped

8–10 kaffir lime leaves, centre vein removed and finely sliced

Mango, cucumber and herb noodle salad
200 g (7 oz) dried rice noodle vermicelli

3 Lebanese cucumbers, cut into long thin ribbons

½ mango (or ruby grapefruit), peeled and sliced into segments

½ bunch coriander (cilantro)

½ bunch mint

½ bunch basil

2 spring onions (scallions), thinly sliced

1 large chili, deseeded and thinly sliced lengthways

Dressing
2 tablespoons lime juice

2 tablespoons gluten free fish sauce

2 teaspoons extra virgin olive oil

METHOD

- To make the marinade, combine all of the ingredients in a bowl. Add seafood and toss to coat. Cover and refrigerate for at least 30 minutes. When ready to cook, thread seafood onto skewers, alternating between the salmon, fish, prawns and squid.

- Meanwhile, cook the noodles for the salad by placing rice vermicelli in a medium bowl and covering completely with boiling water. Cover with plastic wrap and leave for 15–20 minutes or until softened but still al dente. Run under cold water to cool and then drain completely.

- Place cucumber ribbons, mango, coriander, mint, basil, spring onions, chili and cooled vermicelli in a large bowl.

- In a small bowl, combine lime juice, fish sauce and olive oil and pour over the salad. Toss to combine and then divide between bowls.

- Heat a barbecue or grill pan to a high temperature. Sear the seafood skewers until just cooked, about 1 minute on each side. Serve skewers hot.

Note: If you are using bamboo skewers (not metal), soak 8 skewers in water for 30 minutes. If using grapefruit in the salad (instead of mango), add a tablespoon of sweetener (sugar or honey) to counter the fruit's astringency.

SEARED SWORDFISH WITH WASABI, EDAMAME AND AVOCADO SMASH

Sophisticated enough for a Sunday lunch but quick enough for a weeknight supper, the success of this dish relies on creamy avocados and fresh fish. Be careful not to overcook the swordfish—a quick sear on each side is plenty.

INGREDIENTS

1 large ripe avocado, diced
80 g (3 oz) cooked edamame beans, thawed and podded
1 teaspoon wasabi paste, or to taste
100 g (3½ oz) cherry or heirloom tomatoes, quartered
1 ½ tablespoons extra virgin olive oil
4 x 180 g (6¼ oz) swordfish steaks
sea salt and freshly ground black pepper

METHOD

- In a bowl, use the back of a fork to roughly mix together the avocado, edamame and wasabi. Toss through the cherry tomatoes, drizzle with ½ tablespoon of extra virgin olive oil and season to taste.
- Heat a grill to a medium-high temperature.
- Brush the swordfish steaks with 1 tablespoon of extra virgin olive oil and season generously with salt and pepper. Grill the steaks until just cooked through, about 1–2 minutes per side (depending on thickness of steaks).
- Divide avocado smash between bowls and top with swordfish.

Note: To make this paleo, omit the edamame beans.

MAPLE, GREEN TEA AND LEMONGRASS SALMON PARCELS WITH CHARRED VEGETABLES

Cooking in parcels or, as the French say, *en papillote*, yields the most wonderful rewards without much effort. Just throw the ingredients into your DIY paper parcels and let the magic happen—the paper locks in the flavor and moisture. Roasting salmon at a low temperature results in soft and velvety fish (plus, it's a rather forgiving technique as you're unlikely to overcook the fish). Even if you don't enjoy eating salmon skin, that tough, fatty layer protects the fish from drying out (and being overcooked).

INGREDIENTS

1 green tea bag

125 ml (4 fl oz) hot water

2 fresh lemongrass stalks, white part only, finely chopped

1 garlic clove, finely chopped

1 teaspoon ginger, finely grated

1 teaspoon sesame oil

1 tablespoon tamari (or light soy sauce)

1 tablespoon pure maple syrup

4 x 160 g (5½ oz) salmon (or ocean trout) fillets, scaled, skin-on and pin-boned

Steamed Coconut and Spring Onion Brown Rice (p. 193), to serve

Charred vegetables

1 tablespoon extra virgin olive oil

12 asparagus spears, trimmed (or bok choy or broccolini)

4–6 spring onions (scallions), chopped into 5 cm (2 in) batons

2 long red chilies, deseeded and finely sliced lengthways

METHOD

- Preheat oven to 150°C (300°F).
- Seep the green tea bag in hot water for 5 minutes. Remove tea bag and set the tea aside to cool completely.
- Place lemongrass in a mortar and, using the pestle, crush to a paste. Place in a bowl with garlic, ginger, sesame oil, tamari and maple syrup. Add salmon fillets and toss to coat. Add cold tea to the marinating salmon. Leave to marinate for as long as possible, overnight is best.
- Cut 4 large sheets of non-stick baking (parchment) paper and place a salmon fillet in the middle of each. Pour over marinade and fold the paper over, twisting the edges, to create a sealed parcel. Place the parcels on a large roasting tray and cook for 10–15 minutes. To check if the salmon is cooked, insert a fork through the thickest part of the fish and if there's no resistance and the flesh separates easily from the skin, it is ready.
- Meanwhile, to prepare the vegetables, heat a grill pan over a medium-high temperature. Add oil, asparagus, spring onions and chili. Grill until lightly charred, turning occasionally, about 3 minutes.
- Divide rice between bowls, add charred vegetables and pour each parcel on top, allowing the juices to run through the rice.

HARISSA PRAWNS WITH CHARRED CORN, SUGAR SNAP PEA AND BEETROOT SLAW

This tangled slaw is a vibrant medley of sweet corn kernels, crisp raw beetroot and sugar snap peas—tossed in a refreshing lemon and vinegar dressing. This is great for a barbecue as you can do the slaw ahead of time and toss through the dressing at the last minute. I must point out though, the beetroot will run a little—coating all the vegetables in a gorgeous purple hue.

INGREDIENTS

Slaw

2 ears of corn, outer husk and silk (white string) removed, lightly brushed with extra virgin olive oil

¼ red or white cabbage (about 300 g/10½ oz), shredded using a mandolin

2 medium beetroot (any color; about 250 g/9 oz), peeled, julienned using a mandolin

200 g (7 oz) sugar snap peas, thinly sliced on the diagonal

½ bunch coriander (cilantro), roughly chopped

½ bunch mint, roughly chopped

3 spring onions (scallions), finely sliced

Dressing

3 tablespoons extra virgin olive oil

2 tablespoons red wine vinegar

1 tablespoon lemon juice

sea salt and freshly ground pepper

Harissa prawns

1 tablespoon extra virgin olive oil

700 g (1 lb 8 oz) green prawns (shrimp), peeled, deveined and tail intact

1–2 tablespoons Harissa Paste (p. 190) or store-bought harissa paste

Whole Egg Mayonnaise (p. 178), to serve

METHOD

- Heat a char-grill pan or barbecue to a high temperature and when it starts to smoke, add corn. Chargrill for 10–12 minutes, turning so that all sides get some color (this will create quite a lot of smoke and the corn may pop and snap). Remove from the heat and, when cool enough to handle, use a large knife to shave off the corn kernels. Set aside.
- Place shredded cabbage, beets, sugar snap peas, coriander, mint and spring onions in a large bowl.
- Whisk together all the dressing ingredients and season to taste.
- When ready to serve, heat the oil for the harissa prawns in a frying pan to a medium-high temperature. Place prawns in a bowl and toss with harissa. When pan is hot, add prawns, in batches if necessary, and cook for 2 minutes on each side or until just cooked.
- At the last minute, dress the slaw and divide between bowls. Top with harissa prawns and serve immediately with mayonnaise.

Note: To make this paleo, leave out the corn and sugar snap peas.

MISO BUTTER SCALLOPS WITH WATERCRESS AND SOBA NOODLES

Before I moved to London I was so lucky to spend a week with my family on the beautiful North Coast of New South Wales in Australia. Every day we would visit the fish co-op to see what the boats had caught that night. One morning, they had the most gloriously plump scallops. This dish was the result—I didn't want to do too much to the scallops, just toss them in butter then add a dash of miso to caramelize and season.

INGREDIENTS

2 tablespoons brown rice or white (shiro) miso paste
3 tablespoons butter, softened
250 g (9 oz) soba (100 per cent buckwheat) noodles
80 g (3 oz) watercress
4 spring onions (scallions), thinly sliced
16–20 raw scallops, roe removed
2 tablespoons black and white sesame seeds, toasted

Dressing
2 tablespoons tamari (or light soy sauce)
2 tablespoons apple cider vinegar
1 tablespoon sesame oil
1 teaspoon ginger, finely grated

METHOD

- Place miso and 2 tablespoons of butter together in a bowl. Stir to combine and set aside until ready to cook the scallops.
- Bring a saucepan of salted water to the boil. Cook soba, stirring occasionally, for 4–5 minutes or until al dente. Run under cold water to cool and then drain completely.
- Meanwhile, prepare the dressing by combining tamari, vinegar, sesame oil and ginger in a bowl. Pour dressing over cooked and cooled soba noodles and add watercress and spring onions. Toss to combine.
- Add the remaining 1 tablespoon of butter to a large frying pan and heat to a medium temperature. Once the butter has melted and reaches a honey golden color, add the scallops. Cook for 1–2 minutes or until the bottom side is just caramelized. Flip and cook for a further 30 seconds. Add the miso butter to the pan and, using a spoon, coat the scallops with the miso butter. Cook until the scallops have caramelized but are still translucent in the middle, no more than 1–2 minutes.
- Divide soba noodle salad between bowls, top with seared scallops and scatter with sesame seeds. Pour any leftover miso butter from the pan over the scallops.

Note: If you can't get your hands on fresh scallops, prawns makes a wonderful substitute. Use 100 per cent buckwheat soba for a more nutritious and gluten free salad. To make this dairy free, use oil in place of butter.

WOK FRIED JAPANESE BUBBLE AND SQUEAK WITH PRAWNS AND TAMARI MAYONNAISE

This is a cross between a classic British bubble and squeak and okonomiyaki, a Japanese pancake made with shredded cabbage and other grated vegetables. The texture of scrambled egg white can be dry so, to avoid this, just lower the heat of your wok and cook it a little slower.

INGREDIENTS

3 tablespoons rice bran oil (or coconut oil)

2 garlic cloves, finely chopped

¼ white cabbage (about 300 g / 10 oz), finely shredded

3 spring onions (scallions), finely sliced

600 g (1 lb 5 oz) green prawns (shrimp), peeled, deveined and tails intact

10 free range egg whites or 6–8 whole eggs, about 250 ml (8 fl oz), lightly beaten

2 teaspoons gluten free fish sauce

a sprig of coriander (cilantro), to serve

Tamari mayonnaise

3 tablespoons Whole Egg Mayonnaise (p. 178) or store-bought

2 teaspoons tamari (or light soy sauce)

1 teaspoon sesame oil

¼ teaspoon chili powder

METHOD

- Heat 1 tablespoon of oil in a wok to a medium-high temperature. Add the garlic, white cabbage and spring onions and cook until the cabbage has softened and is lightly golden on the edges. Remove from the wok and set aside. Heat another 1 tablespoon of oil to a medium-high temperature and add the prawns. Stir-fry until they just change color (but still translucent in the middle). Remove prawns from the pan and set aside.

- In a bowl, beat egg whites (or whole eggs) and fish sauce until foamy. Add the remaining tablespoon of oil to the wok and heat over a medium-low temperature. Add egg whites, together with the sautéed garlic, cabbage, spring onions and cooked prawns. Cook until egg whites are just set (don't stir too much as it will just become mush—you want it to cook like an omelet).

- Combine all the tamari mayonnaise ingredients in a small bowl.

- Divide bubble and squeak between bowls, drizzle with tamari mayonnaise, scatter with coriander and eat immediately.

Note: With the leftover egg yolks, you can whip up some Whole Egg Mayonnaise (p. 178), the Gooey Chocolate and Espresso Puddings with Salted Almond Brittle (p. 162) or the Peach, White Chocolate and Macadamia Tartlets (p. 170).

SMOKY BARBECUED SQUID
WITH PAPAYA AND TAMARIND SALSA

In the middle of summer, when it almost feels too hot to eat—and I stress the 'almost' part— this is the type of dish I crave. Spicy and fragrant with bold and fresh flavors, this just-seared squid and fresh salsa comes together in a matter of minutes. If you can't source fresh squid, any fresh seafood will do the trick.

INGREDIENTS

4 small, squid (calamari) tubes, cleaned
2 tablespoons extra virgin olive oil
2 garlic cloves, finely chopped
2 teaspoons ground cumin
½ teaspoon smoked paprika
2 teaspoons sea salt
Whole Egg Mayonnaise (p. 178),
    to serve

Papaya and tamarind salsa
½ red papaya or yellow paw paw (about
    400 g/14 oz), peeled, deseeded and
    diced
2 large red chilies, deseeded, thinly
    sliced
2 spring onions (scallions), thinly sliced
½ ripe avocado, diced
½ bunch coriander (cilantro), roughly
    chopped
½ bunch mint, roughly chopped
1 tablespoon tamarind purée
1 tablespoon lime (or lemon) juice
2 teaspoons gluten free fish sauce

METHOD

- For the squid, split the tubes and lay them flat. Score the surface of each tube in a very fine criss-cross pattern. Cut the squid into large irregular triangles. Pat dry with absorbent paper to remove any excess water. Place squid in a bowl and add oil, garlic, cumin, paprika and salt. Toss to combine and set aside until ready to cook.
- To make the salsa, combine the papaya, chili, spring onions, avocado, coriander and mint in a large bowl. In a separate bowl, whisk together tamarind, lime juice and fish sauce. Pour dressing over the salsa mixture and toss to combine.
- Heat the barbecue or grill pan to a high temperature. When the grill is hot, cook squid, turning occasionally, until lightly charred and just cooked, about 2 minutes each side. Serve immediately with papaya and tamarind salsa and mayonnaise.

GREEN CEVICHE

Returning from my honeymoon in Mexico with a fervent love of ceviche, I made it my top priority to recreate it at home. Cooking with fresh, quality produce makes for naturally delicious food in all recipes and this ceviche is certainly a case in point. The freshness of the fish is crucial. While not traditional to do so, I'm an avo-holic so I've included a generous serving of avocado—but please, modify to your taste.

INGREDIENTS

Ceviche
500 g (1 lb 2 oz) firm, fresh fish fillets
    (tuna, barramundi or mahi mahi),
    skin, bones, and bloodline removed
½ teaspoon sea salt
125 ml (4 fl oz) fresh lime juice
1 garlic clove, finely grated
2 teaspoons jalapeño chilies, finely
    chopped
2 ripe avocados, finely diced
2 spring onions (scallions), thinly sliced
1 bunch coriander (cilantro), roughly
    chopped
150 g (5¼ oz) mixed heirloom cherry
    tomatoes, halved and quartered
2 tablespoons extra virgin olive oil, to
    serve
micro greens, to serve
Twice-Cooked Crunchy Garlic Quinoa
    (p. 192), to serve
corn tostadas, toasted tortillas or corn
    chips, to serve

METHOD

- Cut the fish into 1 cm (½ in) cubes and place in a bowl. Add sea salt and lime juice and toss to combine. There should be enough lime juice to just cover the fish. Cover and refrigerate for 15 minutes, stirring gently from time to time. You don't want to leave the fish for too long as it will become chalky and dry.
- Remove fish from the refrigerator and add garlic, jalapeño, avocado, spring onions, coriander and tomatoes. Toss to combine.
- Divide the quinoa between bowls and top with ceviche, drizzle with olive oil and scatter with micro greens. Serve immediately with tostadas.

SPICY BUDGET TUNA POKE
WITH STEAMED GINGER AND CARROT BROWN RICE

While writing this book, two of my best friends, Tess and Henry, got engaged in Hawaii and came home raving about poke. Traditionally, this Hawaiian specialty, pronounced poke-ay, requires sashimi grade fish however sometimes our budgets don't allow for such a luxury nor do some of us have access to such high quality fish. This is when my everyday tuna poke recipe comes into action. If you can get your hands on fresh tuna, halve the dressing and leave out the coriander.

INGREDIENTS

Steamed ginger and carrot brown rice

200 g (7 oz) long grain brown rice

2 carrots, peeled and grated

4 cm (1½ in) ginger, sliced

1 cm (½ in) fresh turmeric or ¼ teaspoon ground
    turmeric

500 ml (16 fl oz) Chicken Broth (p. 187) or water

Tuna poke

1 x 425 g (15 oz) tin good quality tuna in olive oil,
    drained and oil reserved

1 large ripe avocado, diced

6 cherry tomatoes, quartered

2 spring onions (scallions), white part only, finely
    chopped

3 tablespoons fresh coriander (cilantro), roughly
    chopped

1 tablespoon black or white toasted sesame seeds, to
    serve

2 tablespoons pickled ginger, to serve

Spicy poke dressing

1 tablespoon tamari (or light soy sauce)

2 teaspoons white balsamic vinegar (or lime juice)

1 teaspoon toasted sesame oil

1 teaspoon fresh ginger, finely grated

¼ teaspoon ground chili

METHOD

- Start by steaming your brown rice. Wash the rice under cold running water and drain. Place rice, grated carrot, ginger and turmeric in a medium saucepan. Add broth and bring to the boil. Reduce heat to low, cover and simmer until rice is just tender and water has evaporated, about 30–35 minutes. Set aside.

- Place tuna in a large bowl, reserving drained oil. Add avocado, tomatoes, spring onions and coriander. Toss to combine.

- In a small bowl, stir to combine dressing ingredients; tamari, vinegar, sesame oil, ginger and chili.

- Pour dressing over tuna and toss to coat. If the mixture is too dry, add some of the drained tuna oil and toss again.

- Divide steamed rice between the bowls and top with the dressed tuna. Scatter with sesame seeds and pickled ginger.

BLACKENED SALMON BURGER BOWL WITH PICKLED RED ONIONS AND SMOKY CHIPOTLE SAUCE

These bun-less burger bowls are a reminder that healthy eating is downright delicious. Salmon practically swaggers with health benefits, loaded full of omega-3, vitamin D and niacin, plus it's easy to source, wherever you are in the world. The salmon burgers are also delicious the next day so double the batch and save some for lunch the following day.

INGREDIENTS

Cajun spice mix
2 teaspoons paprika
½ teaspoon dried thyme
½ teaspoon garlic powder
½ teaspoon onion powder (optional)
½ teaspoon sea salt
½ teaspoon freshly ground black pepper
¼ teaspoon cayenne pepper

Blackened salmon burger bowl
500 g (1 lb 2 oz) salmon fillet or 4 x
   125 g (4½ oz) salmon pieces, skin off,
   pin-boned and diced
3 spring onions (scallions), thinly sliced
3–4 tablespoons coriander (cilantro),
   finely chopped
2 tablespoons dill, finely chopped
2–3 tablespoons extra virgin olive oil
Sweet Potato Wedges (p. 150), to serve
Pickled Red Onions and Smoky
   Chipotle Sauce (p. 150), to serve

METHOD

- Combine Cajun spice mix ingredients in a small bowl.
- To make the burgers, place diced salmon in a food processor and blend until the salmon breaks down to a mince consistency. Add spring onions, coriander and dill and process until just combined.
- Remove from food processor and divide the salmon mixture into four. Flatten into patties and generously scatter both sides with the Cajun spice mix, about 1 teaspoon per patty.
- Heat a non-stick frying pan over a medium temperature and add olive oil. When hot, cook the patties for 2–3 minutes each side, or until just cooked through. If you do this in batches, use half the oil and repeat.
- Divide the sweet potato wedges between four bowls, top with blackened salmon burgers and pickled red onions. Drizzle with smoky chipotle sauce.

LEMONGRASS AND TURMERIC SEAFOOD CURRY

The star of this fragrant curry is turmeric, one of nature's most powerful healers. With its anti-inflammatory, antioxidant and immune-boosting properties, I try to add a pinch of this intoxicating, bright yellow spice whenever I can. Fresh turmeric, which is sweeter than ground turmeric looks a bit like ginger, except its flesh is orange. Like ginger, turmeric will keep in the freezer for a few months.

INGREDIENTS

200 g (7 oz) long grain brown rice
500 ml (16 fl oz) Chicken Broth (p. 187)
   or stock of choice/water
pinch of salt

Lemongrass turmeric curry paste
2 lemongrass stalks, trimmed, tender centre part only
3 garlic cloves, roughly chopped
2 Asian shallots or 2 golden shallots/¼ small onion, peeled
1 small bird's eye chili, roughly chopped
1 cm (½ in) piece of ginger, peeled
2 teaspoons ground turmeric or 1 cm (½ in) fresh turmeric
1 teaspoon ground cumin
5 kaffir lime leaves, centre vein removed and finely sliced
1 teaspoon lime zest
1 teaspoon rice bran oil

Curry
lemongrass turmeric curry paste (as above)
400 ml (14 fl oz) coconut milk
350 g (12½ oz) green prawns (shrimp), peeled, tails on
350 g (12½ oz) scallops (roe removed)
100 g (3½ oz) snow peas, topped and tailed and outer string removed
1 tablespoon gluten free fish sauce
12 kaffir lime leaves, centre vein removed and finely sliced
2 long red chilies, deseeded and sliced lengthways

METHOD

- Start by steaming your brown rice. Wash rice under cold running water and drain. Place rice, broth and a pinch of salt in a saucepan and bring to the boil. Reduce heat to a low temperature, cover and simmer until rice is just tender and the water has evaporated, about 30–35 minutes. Set aside until ready to eat.
- Place all the paste ingredients in a mortar and pestle and pound to a smooth paste (or use a food processor and blend). If using a mortar and pestle, pound for as long as you can, making sure everything has broken down and combined. Depending on the quality of your food processor, you may need to add some water to blend the ingredients into a paste.
- To prepare the curry, heat a large wok to a medium temperature. Add curry paste and cook, stirring constantly for 3–4 minutes or until lightly golden and fragrant. Stir in the coconut milk, prawns and snow peas and cook for about 1 minute before adding the scallops.
- Pour in the fish sauce and kaffir lime leaves and cook until the scallops and prawns are just cooked (it is better to undercook your seafood, remembering it will continue to cook after you remove the wok from the heat).
- Divide rice between serving bowls, pour over curry and garnish with extra kaffir lime leaves and chili and serve.

Note: Asian shallots are a red, small onion that can be found at most supermarkets or your local Asian greengrocer.

Go with the Grain

This is my favorite chapter in the book. These are recipes for dishes that I eat on a daily basis. On a Sunday night, I try to roast the vegetables left in my refrigerator (any softer-than-it's-meant-to-be beetroot or any forgotten-about-for-weeks sweet potatoes) so that I can quickly and easily whip up dishes such as the Back to The Roots Bowl with Baby Beetroot, Millet and Chili Herb Dressing (p. 71) or the Nourishing Bowl (p. 76).

Grains and carbohydrates in general have developed a bad reputation in recent years and although it is true that processed carbohydrates contain little nutritional value and are absorbed into the blood stream quickly, if you're sensible about the types you choose (such as eating complex carbohydrates in the form of whole grains), carbohydrates can and should make up a healthy and valuable part of your diet. Included in this chapter are seeds such as quinoa, buckwheat and chia seeds that can easily substitute for grains and provide excellent nutritional value.

I tend to mix and match all the dressings and sauces from each of the following dishes—the Avocado Aioli (p. 83) is gorgeous with a simply grilled piece of fish while the Mustard Vinaigrette (p. 76) that I use in the Nourishing Bowl doubles as my everyday salad dressing. Whenever I'm craving something hearty, I smother the creamy tahini dressing from the Poppy Seed-Crusted Sweet Potato (p. 89) over steamed quinoa or brown rice to serve as a side with a roasted chicken or grilled steak.

BACK TO THE ROOTS BOWL WITH BABY BEETROOT, MILLET AND CHILI HERB DRESSING

This is one of my husband's favorite meals. His other favorites include American-style barbecue ribs and hot chips, if that helps to convince you how good this is. Millet is a nutty gluten free grain that has a high amino-acid protein profile and contains more iron than any other cereal grain. The herb dressing in this salad wakes up the flavors of the dish but if you don't like heat, skip the chili flakes.

INGREDIENTS

5–6 fresh colorful baby beetroots, about 500 g (1 lb 2 oz)

200 g (7 oz) millet, rinsed and drained

500 ml (16 fl oz) Chicken Broth (p. 187) or Vegetable Broth (for vegan and vegetarian option, p. 188)

4 red (or watermelon) radishes, finely sliced on a mandolin

Chili herb dressing

1 bunch flat leaf parsley, finely chopped

1 bunch coriander (cilantro), finely chopped

2 garlic cloves, finely chopped or grated on a fine zester

1 teaspoon chili flakes

1 teaspoon Dijon mustard

3 tablespoons extra virgin olive oil

3 tablespoons lemon juice

2 tablespoons red wine vinegar

sea salt and freshly ground black pepper

METHOD

- Preheat oven to 200°C (400°F).
- Wrap each beetroot bulb in foil. Spread out on a baking tray and cook for 45–50 minutes or until tender. The cooking time will differ depending on the size of your beetroot. Check, at intervals, by piercing the beetroot with a skewer—if there is no resistance, the beetroot is cooked.
- While the beetroot is cooking, place the millet and broth in a small saucepan and bring to the boil. Reduce the heat, cover and cook until the liquid has been absorbed and the millet is tender, about 20–25 minutes. Uncover, fluff with a fork and set aside.
- To make the herb dressing, place all the ingredients in a bowl and stir to combine. Taste and adjust seasoning if needed.
- Once beetroot is cooked and is cool enough to handle, use plastic gloves to peel the beetroot. Cut beetroot in half, thinly slice and place in a medium bowl. Add the cooked millet and sliced radishes. Pour over dressing and gently toss to combine. Divide between bowls to serve.

Note: Whenever I make this salad, I triple the dressing to use for salads the following week or to toss over soft boiled eggs for breakfast.

MUSHROOM AND LEEK QUINOA RISOTTO WITH DILL PESTO

I've toyed with this recipe for quite some time, worried that quinoa couldn't replicate the creaminess of Arborio rice. Then I began testing and realised that quinoa is perfect, especially as it's a lot more forgiving than aborio rice (it won't become mush if you overcook it). It is always a challenge to get the right Parmesan-to-butter-to-mushroom-ratio so use this recipe as a guide but trust your tastebuds—and make changes as you see fit. Please, please make the dill pesto. It adds a final fling of flavor that makes this dish.

INGREDIENTS

1 tablespoon extra virgin olive oil

3 tablespoons butter, coarsely chopped

1 large red onion, finely diced

1 leek, white part only, thinly sliced

2 garlic cloves, finely chopped

190 g (6½ oz) quinoa (white, red or tricolor), washed and rinsed

500 ml (16 fl oz) Chicken Broth (p. 187)

300 g (10½ oz) assorted mushrooms, chopped

50 g (1¾ oz) Parmesan, finely grated, plus extra to serve

Dill pesto

½ bunch dill, finely chopped

1 bunch flat leaf parsley, finely chopped

100 ml (3½ fl oz) extra virgin olive oil

50 g (1¾ oz) pumpkin seeds (pepitas), finely chopped

½ lemon, juiced

METHOD

- Heat oil and 1 tablespoon of the butter in a saucepan over a medium-high temperature. Add onion, leek and garlic and cook, stirring occasionally, until lightly golden and tender, about 5 minutes. Add quinoa and stir to coat the grains.
- Pour in the broth and reduce heat to a simmer. Cover and cook until the broth is absorbed and the quinoa is cooked, about 15 minutes.
- Heat the remaining 2 tablespoons of butter in a frying pan to a medium-high temperature. When the butter starts foaming, add chopped mushrooms and stir until the mushrooms are golden and tender, about 5 minutes. Add mushrooms to the 'risotto' and stir to combine.
- To make the pesto, combine all the ingredients in a bowl and season to taste. Alternatively, you can place all the ingredients in a food processor and pulse to combine.
- When ready to serve, add Parmesan to the 'risotto' and stir until thickened slightly, about 2 minutes. Season to taste, divide between bowls and scatter generously with dill pesto.

SICHUAN EGGPLANT WITH STEAMED COCONUT AND SPRING ONION BROWN RICE

This recipe was initially meant to go in my first cookbook, *Bowl & Fork*, but I had too many eggplant recipes (seriously, who doesn't want an entire book dedicated to eggplant?). In hindsight, I'm pleased it didn't go in because I've had time to perfect it. You won't notice the absence of meat but if you can't go without that extra protein hit, toss through some lean pork or chicken mince.

INGREDIENTS

3–4 tablespoons coconut or extra virgin olive oil

500 g (1 lb 2 oz) eggplant (aubergine), sliced into 3 cm (1¼ in) cubes

2 cm (¾ in) piece of ginger, peeled and finely grated

3 garlic cloves, finely chopped

2 Asian shallots (or ½ red onion), peeled and finely diced

1 large red chili, deseeded and thinly sliced

2 teaspoons Sichuan peppercorns, lightly crushed

250 ml (8 fl oz) Chicken Broth (p. 187) or any stock of choice

2 tablespoons dry sherry

1 tablespoon apple cider vinegar

1 tablespoon tamari (or light soy sauce)

1 teaspoon sesame oil

Steamed Coconut and Spring Onion Brown Rice (p. 193), to serve

METHOD

- Add 1 tablespoon of the oil to a large wok and heat to a medium-high temperature. Stir-fry eggplant, in batches, adding 1 tablespoon of oil each time, until the eggplant has softened and has caramelized around the edges. You may need to add a little more oil, depending on the size of your wok. Set aside.
- Add 1 tablespoon of oil to the wok and then stirring constantly, sauté ginger, garlic, shallots and chili until lightly golden. Add Sichuan peppercorns and cook for 1 minute or until fragrant.
- Return the eggplant to the wok and add chicken broth, dry sherry, apple cider vinegar, tamari and sesame oil. Cook for a further 4–5 minutes or until eggplant has softened and absorbed the sauce.
- Divide the rice between bowls and top with eggplant. Serve and eat immediately.

Note: Asian shallots can be found at most supermarkets or your local Asian greengrocer.

KALE AND ALMOND PESTO SPAGHETTI WITH CRISPY PANCETTA BEANS

I usually buy edamame and mung bean fettuccine (available at health food stores and most supermarkets) for this recipe as the noodles are not only gluten free but have a gorgeously nutty flavor that works perfectly with this kale and almond pesto. Feel free to use any pasta of your choice, I've made the dish with normal spaghetti and even rice noodles but the only non-negotiable in this recipe; make the pancetta beans.

INGREDIENTS

Kale pesto
60 g (2 oz) dry roasted almonds (or cashews), unsalted
2 garlic cloves, roughly chopped
125 ml (4 fl oz) extra virgin olive oil
½ bunch (100 g / 3½ oz) green kale, rinsed and dried, ribs and stems removed, thinly sliced
½ bunch flat leaf parsley, roughly chopped
2–3 tablespoons Parmesan cheese, grated
1 large lemon, juiced
sea salt and pepper, to taste

Crispy pancetta beans
1 tablespoon extra virgin olive oil
400 g (14 oz) cooked cannellini beans, rinsed, drained and patted dry
8 slices (75 g/2½ oz) pancetta (gluten free), chopped
400 g (14 oz) spaghetti (gluten free) or buckwheat noodles (see note)
pinch of salt

METHOD

- Place almonds, garlic, olive oil, kale, parsley, Parmesan and lemon juice in a food processor and blitz until smooth. Season to taste and set aside. Don't throw your kale ribs or stems away, once chopped they make a great base for a stir-fry.
- To make the crispy pancetta beans, heat the olive oil in a large non-stick frying pan to a medium temperature. Add drained beans and pancetta and cook, stirring occasionally, until golden brown and crisp, about 10 minutes. The beans may spit and break open a little but just turn down the heat and avoid stirring too much or the beans will become mushy.
- Bring a large saucepan of salted water to the boil. Cook pasta, according to packet instructions, until al dente.
- Place pasta in a large bowl. Add the kale pesto and toss to combine. Divide pasta between serving bowls and top with crispy pancetta beans. Scatter with extra Parmesan and serve.

Note: You can substitute with normal or whole wheat pasta if you can tolerate gluten. To store pesto, put in a container or jar, cover the surface with a little more olive oil and keep in the refrigerator for a week, or freeze for up to a month.

NOURISHING BOWL WITH ROASTED PUMPKIN, QUINOA, CHIA AND MUSTARD VINAIGRETTE

If I had a gun to my head and had to choose my favorite recipe in this book, it would be this. That's a morbid way of highlighting my love of this salad but I'm a pretty indecisive person so the explanation was necessary. It is a great dish to have up your sleeve when cooking for family or friends with dietary requirements as it pleases pretty much everyone (except any paleo-ers).

INGREDIENTS

700 g (1 lb 8 oz) butternut pumpkin (squash), peeled

2 tablespoons extra virgin olive oil

190 g (6½ oz) tricolor quinoa, washed and drained

500 ml (16 fl oz) Vegetable Broth (p. 188) or any stock/broth of choice

3 spring onions (scallions), finely sliced

handful of pea shoots

50 g (1¾ oz) mung, adzuki, lentil and pea sprouts (optional)

few handfuls of coarsely chopped fresh herbs (flat leaf parsley, basil, tarragon and/or dill)

3–4 tablespoons white and black chia seeds

Mustard vinaigrette

80 ml (2¾ fl oz) extra virgin olive oil

3 tablespoons red wine vinegar

1 lemon, juiced

2 tablespoons wholegrain (seeded) mustard

sea salt and freshly ground pepper

METHOD

- Preheat oven to 200°C (400°F).
- Start by roasting the pumpkin. Chop into cubes and place on a baking tray. Add olive oil and toss to coat. Bake for 30–40 minutes (tossing halfway through) or until the pumpkin is tender and golden around the edges. Set aside and allow to cool to room temperature.
- Place quinoa and broth in a small saucepan and bring to the boil. Reduce heat, cover and cook until the liquid has been absorbed and the quinoa is tender, about 15 minutes. Uncover, fluff the quinoa with a fork and set aside to allow to cool.
- Place quinoa in a large bowl. Add roasted pumpkin cubes, spring onions, pea shoots, mixed sprouts (if using), herbs and chia seeds.
- Combine vinaigrette ingredients in a small jug. Drizzle dressing over salad and toss to combine.
- Divide between bowls and scatter with extra chia seeds, to serve.

Note: Whenever I make this, I double the batch for lunch and dinner for the following few days.

NUTTY BROWN RICE DETOX SALAD WITH BLOOD ORANGE VINAIGRETTE

I often forget just how good these simple ingredients taste together, especially if you can get your hands on some sweet, blushing blood oranges. This is my version of a detox salad—far from bland—a zingy, citrus-based dressing full of fresh ginger tossed through with aromatic herbs, nutty brown rice and a crunch of nuts and seeds. If you have some poached or grilled chicken breast on hand, you can add this for a protein boost.

INGREDIENTS

Salad
200 g (7 oz) brown rice, washed and rinsed
500 ml (16 fl oz) water
2 tablespoons pumpkin seeds (pepitas), about 20 g (¾ oz)
2 tablespoons sunflower seeds, about 20 g (¾ oz)
2 tablespoons almonds, about 20 g (¾ oz), roughly chopped
½ bunch flat leaf parsley or micro parsley, roughly chopped
½ bunch mint, roughly chopped
½ small Spanish onion, peeled and finely diced
2 ripe avocados, diced
1 orange, cut into ½ cm (¼ in) thick wheel-shaped slices
1 blood orange, cut into ½ cm (¼ in) thick wheel-shaped slices

Blood orange vinaigrette
1 teaspoon blood orange zest (or orange zest)
3 tablespoons blood orange juice (or orange juice)
2 tablespoons red wine vinegar
1 tablespoon Dijon mustard
2–3 cm (¾–1¼ in) ginger, finely grated
¼ teaspoon sea salt
125 ml (4 fl oz) extra virgin olive oil

METHOD

- Start by steaming your brown rice. Place rice, water and a pinch of salt in a saucepan and bring to the boil. Reduce heat to low, cover and simmer until rice is just tender and the water has evaporated, about 30–35 minutes. Set aside and allow to cool to room temperature.
- Meanwhile, prepare the seeds. Heat a small non-stick frying pan over a low temperature. Add pumpkin seeds, sunflower seeds and almonds and dry roast, stirring regularly, until lightly golden. Set aside until ready to serve.
- To make the vinaigrette, whisk together the blood orange zest, juice, vinegar, Dijon, ginger and salt in a small bowl. Slowly whisk in the olive oil until the dressing is thick.
- When ready to serve, place cooled rice in a large bowl, add flat leaf parsley, mint, onion and avocado. Drizzle over vinaigrette and toss to combine.
- Divide rice between bowls and top with orange and blood orange wheels and toasted seeds and nuts.

Note: You can substitute uncooked rice with 600 g (1 lb 5 oz) cooked brown rice and skip step 1. If blood oranges are out of season, substitute with any citrus fruit such as ruby grapefruit, tangelo, mandarin or orange.

SUMMER IN A BOWL
WITH MANGO AND HERBED QUINOA

Mango, mint and lime—these ingredients take me right back home to summer in Australia. The simplicity of this salad is what I love about it. If mango or papaya isn't in season, kiwifruit or grapefruit offer a tartness that works surprisingly well. Serve this alongside some fresh, cooked prawns and dollops of Whole Egg Mayonnaise (p. 178).

INGREDIENTS

190 g (6½ oz) quinoa (white, red or tricolor), rinsed and drained

500 ml (16 fl oz) Vegetable Broth (p. 188), water or any stock/broth of choice

1 ripe mango, diced into 1 cm (½ in) cubes

1 ripe avocado, diced into 1 cm (½ in) cubes

2 spring onions (scallions), finely chopped

1 bunch coriander (cilantro) leaves, roughly chopped

1 bunch mint leaves, roughly chopped

2 tablespoons white and/or black sesame seeds, dry roasted

Lemon tamari dressing

2 lemons, juiced

1 tablespoon tamari (or light soy sauce)

1 teaspoon toasted sesame oil

sea salt and freshly ground black pepper

METHOD

- Start by steaming the quinoa. Place quinoa and broth in a small saucepan and bring to the boil. Reduce heat, cover and cook until the liquid has been absorbed and the quinoa is tender, about 15 minutes. Uncover, fluff the quinoa with a fork and set aside to cool completely.
- Meanwhile, place diced mango, diced avocado, spring onions, coriander, mint and sesame seeds in a bowl. Once quinoa has cooled, add to the bowl and toss to combine.
- Combine all the dressing ingredients and pour over salad. Gently toss to combine and divide between bowls. Scatter with extra sesame seeds, to serve.

Note: If making this ahead of time, leave the avocado and herbs out and toss them through just before serving.

RAINBOW GINGER FRIED WILD RICE
WITH GARLIC CHIPS

This is fried rice but not as you know it—rainbow colored vegetables are pepped up with copious amounts of ginger and earthy grains of wild rice. Despite its name, wild rice is not rice at all—it is a semi-aquatic grass with a nutty taste and a chewy texture. Wild rice is a lighter and less carb-dense alternative, which allows the veggies to shine. This is delicious served with the Smoky Spiced Beef Skewers with Tandoori Cashew Sauce (p. 120).

INGREDIENTS

200 g (7 oz) wild rice, washed and rinsed
500 ml (16 fl oz) Vegetable Broth (p. 188)
    or water

Garlic chips
6 garlic cloves
rice bran oil (or coconut oil)

Fried rice
2 tablespoons rice bran oil (or any neutral
    oil)
4 free range eggs, lightly beaten
1 red onion, peeled and finely diced
½ red capsicum (bell pepper), diced
1 zucchini (courgette), diced
2 carrots, peeled and diced
100 g (3½ oz) edamame beans or green
    peas, frozen or fresh, podded
1 ear of corn, outer husk and silk removed
    and kernels shaved off (optional)
4 cm (1½ in) fresh ginger, finely grated
1 long red chili, deseeded and thinly sliced
2 tablespoons tamari (or light soy sauce)
1 tablespoon gluten free fish sauce
1 tablespoon sesame oil
salt and pepper, to taste

METHOD

- Place the wild rice and broth in a saucepan and bring to the boil. Reduce heat to a simmer, cover and cook until tender, about 40–45 minutes. Remove from the heat and allow to stand for 10 minutes. The rice should be chewy and some of the grains will have burst open.
- Meanwhile, make the garlic chips. Peel and slice garlic very thinly. Pour enough oil into a small frying pan or saucepan until it is just over 1 cm (½ in) deep. Heat to a medium-low temperature and add garlic. Simmer, stirring constantly, until the garlic is golden, about 5–6 minutes. Using a slotted spoon, remove garlic and drain on a paper towel. Sprinkle with a pinch of sea salt and set aside to crisp up and cool.
- To cook the fried rice, heat half the oil (1 tablespoon) in a wok or frying pan until just smoking. Add the eggs and gently move them around the wok until just set. Transfer the eggs to a cutting board and roughly chop into pieces. Set aside.
- Heat the remaining oil (1 tablespoon) in the same wok or frying pan to a medium-high temperature. Add the onion, capsicum, zucchini, carrot, beans and corn (if using) and sauté for 2–3 minutes or until the vegetables have softened. Stir in the ginger and chili and cook for a further 2–3 minutes, before adding the wild rice.
- Stir through tamari, fish sauce and sesame oil. Toss through chopped egg and season to taste. Divide between bowls, scatter with garlic chips and serve immediately.

Note: Omit fish sauce to make this vegetarian. Keep any leftover garlic-infused oil (from making the garlic chips) to use in salad dressing.

SPICED QUINOA AND ZUCCHINI PATTIES WITH AVOCADO AIOLI

If you have leftover quinoa in the refrigerator, this makes a quick and healthy midweek meal that doubles as a great lunch to take to work the next day. The avocado aioli has the smoothness of whipped cream and a rich, depth of flavor that makes it quite special—it is equally useful on a cheese platter, as part of a Mexican feast or lathered onto a sandwich or cracker.

INGREDIENTS

100 g (3½ oz) quinoa, rinsed and
   drained (or 230 g (8 oz) cooked
   quinoa)
250 ml (8 fl oz) Vegetable Broth (p. 188)
   or water
3 medium zucchini (courgette), about
   300 g (10½ oz), grated
1 teaspoon sea salt
3 garlic cloves, finely chopped
1 teaspoon ground cumin
¼ teaspoon ground chili
2 spring onions (scallions), finely
   chopped
2 tablespoons coriander (cilantro),
   chopped
1 free range egg, lightly beaten
sea salt and freshly ground pepper
100 g (3½ oz) mixed salad greens, to
   serve

Avocado aioli
1 large ripe avocado, roughly diced
2 garlic cloves, roughly chopped
2 teaspoons lemon juice
1 teaspoon Dijon mustard
3 tablespoons extra virgin olive oil
sea salt and pepper to taste

METHOD

- Preheat oven to 200°C (400°F).
- Start by cooking the quinoa (if not using precooked quinoa). Place quinoa and broth in a small saucepan and bring to the boil. Reduce heat, cover and cook until the liquid has been absorbed and the quinoa is tender, about 15 minutes. Uncover, fluff the quinoa with a fork and set aside.
- Place grated zucchini in a colander set over a bowl and sprinkle with salt. Leave for 10–15 minutes, allowing the salt to extract all the liquid from the zucchini. With clean hands, squeeze any excess liquid from the zucchini, then pat dry with absorbent paper.
- In a bowl, stir to combine the garlic, cumin, chili, spring onions, coriander, egg, cooled quinoa and drained zucchini. Season to taste. If the mixture is too dry and doesn't come together, add another egg. Be mindful that you don't want too much liquid.
- Form the mixture into 5 cm (2 in) diameter by 1 cm (½ in) thick disks and place them on a lined baking tray. It should make about 15 patties. Place in the oven and cook for 20 minutes or until lightly golden.
- Meanwhile, to make the aioli, place the avocado, garlic, lemon juice and mustard in a food processor. Pulse for a few seconds until smooth. Gradually add oil, processing until smooth. Depending on the ripeness of your avocado, you may need to add a dash more oil. Season to taste.
- Divide salad greens between bowls, top with quinoa patties and aioli. Sprinkle with extra chili powder (if desired).

Note: Salad greens can include baby spinach, rocket, curly endive and mizuna (a type of lettuce).

BENTO BOWL WITH MISO GLAZED SALMON, EDAMAME AND SESAME BUCKWHEAT

When I'm tired of brown rice and quinoa, buckwheat is a refreshing change especially when infused with tamari, sesame oil and ginger. Though the recipe is for 4, when I'm dining solo, this is my special, home alone treat.

INGREDIENTS

Sesame buckwheat
200 g (7 oz) raw buckwheat,
  washed and drained
750 ml (1¼ pt) water
1 tablespoon tamari (or light soy sauce)
1 teaspoon sesame oil
1 cm (½ in) fresh ginger, finely grated

Miso glazed salmon
1 tablespoons brown rice or white
  (shiro) miso paste
1 tablespoon pure maple syrup
4 x 180 g (6¼ oz) salmon fillets, skin on
1 tablespoon coconut oil (or olive oil)

Toppings
200 g (7 oz) cooked edamame beans,
  podded
½ cucumber, thinly sliced lengthways into
  ribbons
2 spring onions (scallions), finely sliced
1 tablespoon black and white sesame seeds
1 ripe avocado, thinly sliced
2 tablespoons pickled ginger, store-bought
large handful mixed baby greens

METHOD

- Place buckwheat and water in a saucepan and bring to the boil. Reduce heat, cover and cook until al dente, about 20–25 minutes. Place in a bowl and toss with tamari, sesame oil and ginger. Set aside until ready to eat.
- Combine miso and maple syrup in a large bowl. Add salmon and toss to coat.
- In a non-stick frying pan, heat coconut oil to a medium-high temperature. Cook salmon, skin side down, until skin is charred. Flip over and cook on the other side. The middle should be pink but the outside caramelized. Depending on the size of your frying pan, you may need to cook the salmon in batches.
- To assemble bento bowls, divide buckwheat between bowls, add salmon and top with edamame, cucumber, spring onions, sesame seeds, avocado, pickled ginger and baby green herbs.

Note: Always cook your salmon skin side down first. The skin protects the fish flesh and will help avoid overcooking your salmon. Salad greens can include baby spinach, rocket (arugula), curly endive and mizuna.

SOY AND BALSAMIC TOFU WITH SEEDY FORBIDDEN RICE AND SAUTÉED BROCCOLINI

This salty, sweet dish is a jumble of contrasting tastes and textures that becomes addictive. On first bite, it does taste different but by the end of the bowl, you're scraping the bottom for more. Forbidden (black rice), an heirloom variety chock-full of antioxidants, is rich in iron and fibre and tastes absolutely delicious. You can buy it at most supermarkets however you can easily substitute with brown or red rice—they offer the same nuttiness (and nutritional value).

INGREDIENTS

Seedy forbidden rice
285 g (10 oz) uncooked forbidden rice
200 ml (7 oz) coconut milk
600 ml (1¼ pt) water
½ teaspoon sea salt
3 tablespoons chia seeds
3 tablespoons sunflower seeds, dry roasted
3 tablespoons pumpkin seeds (pepitas), dry roasted

Soy and balsamic tofu
2 tablespoons tamari (or light soy sauce)
1 tablespoon balsamic vinegar
1 tablespoon pure maple syrup
1 tablespoon extra virgin olive oil
½ teaspoon sesame oil
pinch of chili flakes (optional)
375 g (13 oz) firm, fresh tofu (or tempeh), drained, patted dry and cut into thick rectangles

Sautéed broccolini
2 teaspoons extra virgin olive oil
1 bunch broccolini, woody ends trimmed

METHOD

- To cook the rice, wash under cold running water and drain. Place the rice in a saucepan with coconut milk, water and sea salt. Bring to the boil, then reduce heat to a simmer. Cover and cook for 35 minutes or until rice is cooked. Remove from the heat and allow to stand, covered, for 5 minutes. The rice should be soft, yet slightly chewy.
- Prepare the tofu marinade by whisking together the tamari, balsamic vinegar, maple syrup, olive oil, sesame oil and chili flakes (if using) in a shallow bowl. Add tofu rectangles, toss to coat, cover with plastic wrap and set aside until you are ready to cook.
- For the sautéed broccolini, heat oil a non-stick frying pan or grill pan to a high temperature. Add broccolini and cook for 1 minute or until the edges are slightly charred, tossing constantly to coat with oil. Remove from the pan, set aside and keep warm.
- Using the same frying pan, add tofu pieces, in batches, and cook until caramelized and char-grilled. Reserve remaining marinade to serve.
- Toss chia seeds, sunflower seeds and pumpkin seeds through the rice. Divide between bowls, top with caramelized tofu, sautéed broccolini and drizzle over any leftover marinade.

YIN AND YANG BOWL WITH POPPY SEED-CRUSTED SWEET POTATO, LENTIL AND RED RICE SALAD WITH CREAMY TAHINI DRESSING

This bowl is the perfect balance of carbohydrate, fat and protein. In the same way that we understand yin and yang in everyday life, these ingredients come together to create something that is far greater (and more delicious) than the individual parts. Poppy seeds are mostly used in cakes and muffins but here, they create a beautiful crust for the sweet potato. They have a mild, woody taste, which balances the sweetness of the red rice and sweet potato.

INGREDIENTS

600 g (1 lb 5 oz) orange sweet potato, peeled (see note)

2 tablespoons extra virgin olive oil

2 tablespoons poppy seeds

140 g (5 oz) red rice, rinsed and drained

375 ml (12 fl oz) water

1 x 400 g (14 oz) tin brown lentils, rinsed and drained

50 g (1¾ oz) baby rocket (arugula)

small bunch coriander (cilantro) (or other herb of choice), roughly chopped

¼ Spanish onion, thinly sliced lengthways

Creamy tahini dressing

3 tablespoons extra virgin olive oil

3 tablespoons apple cider vinegar

3 tablespoons tahini (see note)

½ teaspoon chili flakes

1 teaspoon sea salt

2 tablespoons water

METHOD

- Preheat oven to 200°C (400°F).
- Start by roasting the sweet potato. Slice into 2 x 3 cm (¾ x 1¼ in) pieces and place on a large baking tray. Add olive oil and poppy seeds and toss to coat. Bake for 35–40 minutes or until lightly golden.
- In a small saucepan, combine the red rice and water. Bring to the boil and then cover, reduce the heat and cook until rice is tender, about 25–30 minutes. Set aside to cool for about 5 minutes and then fluff with a fork.
- Combine dressing ingredients in a small bowl and stir to combine.
- Place cooled red rice in a large bowl. Add roasted sweet potato, drained lentils, rocket, coriander and sliced Spanish onion. Pour over dressing and toss to combine.
- Season to taste and scatter with extra coriander, to serve.

Note: Don't throw away the sweet potato peel, place them on a separate tray with a little oil and roast for 5–10 minutes and eat them as a snack. I have used normal tahini however you can also use black tahini, which gives the salad a wonderful, dramatic color. Tahini tends to separate as it sits (especially if left in the refrigerator)----the oil floats to the top and the paste sinks. The easiest way to combine the oil and paste is to sit the jar upside down for 15 minutes or so before you use the tahini.

Plant
Power

I have always preferred cooking vegetables and this was well before I was aware of the health and environmental benefits of a plant-based diet. To me, there seems to be fewer culinary restrictions when cooking plants and they're more forgiving (there's no fear of undercooking the chicken or forgetting to rest a rib eye!). Don't get me wrong, I enjoy meat but I shy away from cooking it on a daily basis. Instead, I'm drawn to the limitless possibilities of cooking, say, a cauliflower.

As to the health benefits, Michael Pollan, an American journalist, author and activist, has a back-to-basics philosophy that makes sense to me. One of his most oft-quoted sayings is 'Eat food, not too much, mostly plants.' I wish I could say I was more diligent on the 'not too much' part but I do believe in eating largely a plant-based diet. Plant foods are the richest, most bountiful sources of vitamins and minerals. They contain hundreds of thousands of phytochemicals and many of these contain disease-fighting properties that no laboratory could ever duplicate.

While not all vegetarian, the following recipes in this chapter feature plants as the star of the bowl. The Roasted Cherry Tomato and Eggplant Tabbouleh with Garlicky Hummus Dressing (p. 94) is a celebration of Middle Eastern flavors and is one my family's favorite dishes. The Crunchy Cauliflower Salad with Mango, Lime and Jalapeño Dressing (p. 100) is like a Mexican fiesta in your mouth and my Thai Coconut Zucchini Noodles with Prawns and Cashews (p. 103) is a healthy answer to weekday takeaway cravings. It is both simple

FIVE SPICE KENTUCKY FRIED TOFU WITH HONEY MISO SLAW

This recipe uses tofu as it is readily available. However, if you can get your hands on tempeh, it's worth it. Tempeh is made from whole, fermented soybeans and while it has a similar texture and flavor to tofu, it is nutritionally superior; it is higher in fibre and a great source of iron. The key to a great slaw is slicing the veggies super thin. I'm not one for unnecessary kitchen gadgets but nothing really beats a mandolin.

INGREDIENTS

Slaw
½ bunch Tuscan or curly kale, washed and drained
½ red cabbage (about 200 g/7 oz), finely shredded
   on a mandolin
2 carrots, peeled and cut into noodles using a spiralizer (or grated)
½ bunch coriander (cilantro), roughly chopped
3 spring onions (scallions), white part, finely chopped

Honey miso dressing
1 tablespoon brown rice or white (shiro) miso paste
3–4 tablespoons extra virgin olive oil
2 tablespoons white wine vinegar
1 teaspoon toasted sesame oil
1–2 teaspoons runny honey (or pure maple syrup, if vegan)
sea salt and freshly ground pepper

Five spice Kentucky fried tofu
1 teaspoon sesame seeds
1 teaspoon five spice powder
½ teaspoon ground cumin
½ teaspoon turmeric
½ teaspoon black pepper
½ teaspoon sea salt
¼ teaspoon chili powder
375 g (13 oz) firm, fresh tofu or tempeh, drained,
   patted dry and cut into thick rectangles
3 tablespoons extra virgin olive oil

METHOD

- Use a sharp knife to cut out the ribs of the kale leaves. Roll the de-ribbed leaves into a tight cigar shape and thinly slice into ribbons. Transfer the kale to a medium-sized serving bowl. Add the shredded cabbage, carrots, coriander and spring onions.
- In a bowl, whisk to combine dressing ingredients.
- Add the dressing to the kale salad, and, using your hands, gently massage the dressing to coat all the leaves. The key to this salad is to massage the kale—use your hands to rub the dressing into the leaves as this softens them. If you can leave the salad for 20 minutes at this point, the kale will absorb the dressing.
- To make the tofu, place the sesame seeds and all the spices in a shallow bowl. In a separate bowl, place tofu rectangles and toss with olive oil. Then dip each tofu triangle in the spice mix.
- In a large non-stick frying pan, fry tofu (in batches) until golden and crunchy, about 2 minutes on each side.
- Divide slaw between bowls and top with crisp tofu.

Note: Use a spiralizer or mandolin to create carrot 'noodles'.

ROASTED CHERRY TOMATO AND EGGPLANT TABBOULEH WITH GARLICKY HUMMUS DRESSING

I'm one of those people who always has a snack tucked in my handbag (much to husband's embarrassment). Whether it is a handful of nuts, fruit or a Tupperware container of a salad like this. This is one of my go-to dishes because it gets better the day after, is full of protein and travels easily. Wherever I am, I happily pull out a plastic fork and snack away and, despite his embarrassment, Andrew is usually the one to finish off the container!

INGREDIENTS

4 small Lebanese or 2 large eggplants
  (aubergines), about 700 g (1 lb 8 oz)
3 tablespoons extra virgin olive oil
sea salt, to taste
500 g (1 lb 2 oz) cherry tomatoes, on
  the vine
190 g (6½ oz) quinoa (white, red or
  tricolor), rinsed and drained
500 ml (16 fl oz) Vegetable Stock
  (p. 188) or water
2 bunches flat leaf parsley, washed,
  dried and roughly chopped
1 bunch mint leaves, roughly chopped
2 spring onions (scallions), thinly sliced
2 tablespoons Beetroot Tzatziki
  (p. 186), to serve

Garlicky hummus dressing
4 tablespoons extra virgin olive oil
2 lemons, juiced
2 tablespoons Quick Garlicky Hummus
  (p. 185) or store-bought

METHOD

- Preheat oven to 200°C (400°F).
- Start by roasting the eggplant. If using Lebanese eggplants, halve lengthways or, if using normal eggplant, cut into 2 cm (¾ in) thick slices. Place on a tray lined with baking (parchment) paper, drizzle with 2 tablespoons of the olive oil and season with salt.
- On another tray, place the cherry tomatoes and drizzle with the remaining 1 tablespoon olive oil. Season with salt. Place both trays in the oven and roast until the eggplant is browned and tender and the tomatoes are slightly dried at the edges, about 30–35 minutes.
- Place quinoa and broth in a small saucepan and bring to the boil. Reduce heat, cover and cook until the liquid has been absorbed and the quinoa is tender, about 15 minutes. Uncover, fluff the quinoa with a fork and transfer to a large bowl to allow to cool. Once cool, add half the roasted cherry tomatoes, parsley, mint and spring onions.
- Combine dressing ingredients in a small bowl and season to taste. Pour dressing over quinoa mixture. Toss to combine and set aside to allow the flavors to marinate.
- When ready to serve, divide tabbouleh between bowls, top with the remaining roasted cherry tomatoes and eggplant rounds. Serve with an extra dollop of hummus and beetroot tzatziki.

WHOLE ROASTED SPICED CAULIFLOWER WITH TAHINI YOGURT DRESSING

This recipe began life as a whole roasted cauliflower, until I discovered romanesco in all its green, spiky glory. An edible flower bud, romanesco is closely related to cauliflower, broccoli and Brussels sprouts and it responds wonderfully to roasting (much like all brassicas). As cauliflower is more accessible, I have suggested this first but if you can get your hands on romanesco, please do. At least once a week, you will find me perched at my kitchen table wolfing this down.

INGREDIENTS

1 large cauliflower or 2 small romanesco, about 1 kg (2 lb) in total
80 ml (2¾ fl oz) extra virgin olive oil
2 tablespoons sea salt
1 teaspoon ground turmeric
1 teaspoon sweet paprika
1 teaspoon ground cumin
4 garlic cloves, thinly sliced

Tahini yogurt dressing
2 tablespoons tahini paste
2 garlic cloves, finely chopped
200 g (7 oz) natural Greek yogurt
1 lemon, juiced
sea salt and freshly ground pepper
¼ bunch coriander (cilantro), to garnish

METHOD

- Preheat oven to 200°C (400°F).
- On a cutting board, quarter the cauliflower or romanesco, leaving the core and leaves intact. (If using a small cauliflower, simply halve, not quarter.) Transfer the quarters to a large bowl and rub with the olive oil, salt, turmeric, paprika, cumin and garlic.
- Arrange cauliflower on a lined baking tray and roast until tender at the core and lightly browned on the outside, about 35–40 minutes.
- Meanwhile, make the tahini yogurt dressing. Place the tahini, garlic, yogurt and lemon juice in a small bowl. Stir to combine and season to taste.
- Once the cauliflower is cooked, heat the grill and cook the cauliflower until lightly golden and crunchy on the top, about 2–3 minutes.
- Remove the cauliflower from the grill and transfer to a serving bowl. Pour the dressing over the cauliflower, scatter with coriander and devour while hot.

Note: To make this dairy free and paleo, replace the yogurt with coconut yogurt.

SHAVED FENNEL AND CRUSHED MACADAMIA SALAD WITH CONFIT GARLIC DRESSING

I can't tell you how many times I have made this salad. It began with pecans, not macadamias, then it was roasted fennel, not raw. Here is the latest version and by gosh, it's good. The confit garlic dressing is rich and oily—which is just what the sharpness of the fennel is crying out for. The macadamias add a creamy assertiveness that ties it all together. I suggest serving it alongside a simple pasta or soup such as the Curried Pumpkin Soup (p. 33).

INGREDIENTS

Confit garlic dressing
8 garlic cloves
125 ml (4 fl oz) extra virgin olive oil
1 tablespoon sumac
2 lemons, juiced

Salad
100 g (3½ oz) macadamias
2 medium fennel bulbs, finely sliced or shaved, fronds reserved
60 g (2 oz) baby rocket (arugula)
½ bunch mint, roughly chopped
sea salt and freshly ground black pepper

METHOD

- Preheat oven to 180°C (350°F).
- To make the dressing, place garlic and extra virgin olive oil in a small saucepan. The garlic must be submerged so depending on the size of your saucepan, you may need to add a little more oil. Cook over low heat for 30 minutes or until the garlic has softened. Set aside to cool. Place both the garlic and oil in a small bowl and, using the back of a fork, mash the garlic to create a paste. Add the sumac and lemon juice and stir to combine. Season to taste.
- Meanwhile, spread macadamias evenly on a baking tray. Roast for 10 minutes or until lightly golden. Remove from oven and allow to cool. Roughly pound in a mortar and pestle until crumbly but not a powder. Set aside.
- Roughly chop reserved fennel fronds. Place fennel, fronds, rocket, mint and half the macadamias in a bowl. Pour the dressing over and toss to combine.
- Scatter with remaining macadamias and extra sumac, to serve.

Note: The term, confit, is a technique whereby meat (usually duck) is cooked in its own fat at a low temperature. Here, we confit garlic in olive oil to create a soft, delicate and sweet dressing.

ISRAELI CHOPPED SALAD
WITH SCATTERED GOAT'S CHEESE AND ALMONDS

This traditional Israeli salad is a melange of fresh, simple ingredients that packs up well for a picnic (just take the goat's cheese and almonds to scatter on top before you serve). For some, goat's dairy is easier to digest than cow's dairy as it has lower levels of lactose and a protein structure that can be gentler to absorb. This salad is also delicious served with Sumac Lamb Chops (p. 133).

INGREDIENTS

½ bunch coriander (cilantro), finely chopped

½ bunch mint, finely chopped

½ bunch flat leaf parsley, finely chopped

1 large white onion, peeled and finely diced

4 garlic cloves, finely grated

1 large red chili, deseeded, and finely chopped

2 teaspoons ground sumac

1 teaspoon ground cinnamon

125 ml (4 fl oz) extra virgin olive oil

6 spring onions (scallions), thinly sliced

4 medium ripe tomatoes, finely diced

3 small Lebanese cucumbers, seeds removed and finely diced

2 red or watermelon radishes, finely sliced using a mandolin

2 lemons, juiced

2 teaspoons lemon zest

sea salt and freshly ground black pepper, to taste

100 g (3½ oz) goat's cheese, goat's feta, feta or Labneh (p. 183)

60 g (2 oz) dry roasted almonds, roughly chopped

METHOD

- Place all the ingredients (except for the goat's cheese and almonds) in a large bowl. Toss to combine and allow to marinate for at least 20 minutes before serving.
- Divide between bowls and scatter with goat's cheese and almonds.

Note: To make this dairy free and paleo, skip the goat's cheese, feta or labneh.

CRUNCHY CAULIFLOWER SALAD
WITH MANGO, LIME AND JALAPEÑO DRESSING

I have the same affection for roasted cauliflower as I do for coffee and sweet potato wedges. Don't throw away the cauliflower stem—chop it up and throw it in with the florets; it crisps up beautifully when you roast it. In winter, I make this dressing without the mango. Just add another tablespoon or two of olive oil.

INGREDIENTS

1 large cauliflower head (1 kg / 2 lb in total), broken into small florets

3–4 tablespoons extra virgin olive oil

1 teaspoon sea salt

150 g (5¼ oz) baby spinach leaves

2 spring onions (scallions), finely sliced

1 ripe avocado, diced

½ bunch coriander (cilantro), roughly copped

½ bunch mint, roughly chopped

seeds (arils) from ½ pomegranate (optional)

Mango, lime and jalapeño dressing

2 pickled jalapeños, finely chopped

1 mango, roughly diced

2 medium limes, juiced

3 tablespoons extra virgin olive oil

sea salt and freshly ground black pepper

METHOD

- To cook the cauliflower, heat half the oil in a heavy-based frying pan to a medium-high temperature. In batches, cook the cauliflower florets, adding a little more oil with each batch, making sure not to overcrowd the pan. Cook for 6–10 minutes, turning so they color evenly. Once golden, transfer to a plate with absorbent paper and sprinkle with a little salt. Repeat with remaining cauliflower. You may need to add more oil to get the cauliflower golden and crunchy. Alternatively, you can roast your cauliflower in the oven. Preheat oven to 180°C (350°F), toss cauliflower with oil and spread in a single layer on a baking tray. Roast for 40 minutes, tossing occasionally, or until lightly golden. Allow to cool to room temperature.
- Place all dressing ingredients in a food processor and blend until mango has puréed and combined. Season to taste.
- Place spinach leaves, spring onions, avocado, coriander, mint and cooled crunchy cauliflower florets in a large bowl. Add dressing and toss to combine.
- Divide between bowls and top with pomegranate arils (if using).

ALL THINGS GREEN WITH SWEET SESAME SAUCE

One of my favorite Japanese dishes is *goma-ae*, a side dish that is made with steamed spinach and a sesame dressing. While far from traditional, this is my version that uses white balsamic vinegar together with tahini and miso to create an addictive sesame sauce.

INGREDIENTS

1 bunch broccolini (or broccoli), woody ends trimmed
12 French beans
12 snow peas, topped and tailed
12 asparagus spears, woody ends trimmed
1 tablespoon sesame seeds, toasted, to serve

Sweet sesame sauce
3 tablespoons tahini
1 tablespoon brown rice or white (shiro) miso paste
1 tablespoon white balsamic vinegar (or rice wine vinegar)
1 small garlic clove, finely chopped
1 teaspoon tamari (or light soy sauce)
3–4 tablespoons water
sea salt

METHOD

- Bring a large saucepan of salted water to the boil. Add the broccolini and cook for 2 minutes or until just blanched. Use a slotted spoon to remove, drain and set aside. Add the beans and cook for 1 minute (or less). Remove, drain and set aside. Next, add snow peas and asparagus. Cook for 1 minute. Remove, drain well and then dry the asparagus with a clean kitchen tea towel.
- Meanwhile, combine the tahini, miso, vinegar, garlic and tamari in a small bowl. Add water, a tablespoon at a time, to thin until you reach your ideal consistency (it should be pourable but not too runny).
- Place blanched broccolini, beans, snow peas and asparagus in a large bowl. Pour over the dressing and toss to coat. Scatter with sesame seeds, to serve.

THAI COCONUT ZUCCHINI NOODLES WITH PRAWNS AND CASHEWS

Make this recipe when you're craving Thai takeaway but don't want to wake up in the middle of the night, dying of thirst (does this happen to anyone else?). It's important not to crowd the pan when making these noodles, which is why this recipe only serves two (plus it's a bit of a pain to spiralize or slice more than 6 zucchinis at a time). You can add more coconut milk if you'd prefer a more soup-like consistency.

INGREDIENTS

4–6 medium zucchini (courgette), about 500 g (1 lb)

4 tablespoons coconut or rice bran oil

1 long red chili, thinly sliced and deseeded if you don't like heat

2 garlic cloves, finely chopped

300 g (10½ oz) green prawns (shrimp), cleaned, shelled and deveined

1 tablespoon tamari (or light soy sauce)

1 teaspoon gluten free fish sauce

½ teaspoon sesame oil

¼ teaspoon freshly ground black pepper

½ bunch basil, leaves picked

125 ml (4 fl oz) coconut milk

50 g (1¾ oz) unsalted dry roasted cashew nuts

1 lime, quartered, to serve

METHOD

- Cut the zucchinis into wide noodle strips with a spiralizer/mandolin or vegetable peeler.
- Heat half the oil in a wok until smoking, add zucchini noodles and stir-fry for 7–8 minutes or until lightly golden around the edges and just soft. Remove and set aside. You may need to do this in batches, depending on how big your wok is. Try not to overcrowd the pan as the zucchini noodles will sweat.
- Heat the remaining oil in the wok to a high temperature and add the chili. Stir-fry for 1 minute before adding the garlic and stir-fry for another minute. Add the prawns to the wok and cook until the prawns become opaque, about 1–2 minutes.
- Add tamari, fish sauce, sesame oil, pepper and zucchini noodles and toss to combine. Finally, add basil and coconut milk and stir until basil wilts.
- Divide between bowls, scatter with cashew nuts and serve with lime wedges.

ROAST PUMPKIN, BABY CARROTS AND KALE WITH CARROT TOP, PARSLEY AND ANCHOVY PISTOU

For my family, roasted vegetables are the ultimate comfort food. Almost any vegetable tastes delicious when properly roasted—and the type of 'proper' roasting I'm talking about is when the veggies have reached a deep golden brown, with crisp caramelized edges and where the inside is still soft. I always have grand plans to make an extra batch for salads over the week but somehow, despite doubling and tripling the quantities, this dish never makes it that far.

INGREDIENTS

8 baby (heirloom) carrots, brushed clean
600 g (1 lb 5 oz) Japanese pumpkin (squash), cut into 1 cm (½ in) thick wedges
3 tablespoons extra virgin olive oil
½ teaspoon sea salt
½ bunch curly or Tuscan kale, centre vein removed and roughly chopped

Pistou
handful of carrot tops, finely chopped
½ bunch of flat leaf parsley, finely chopped
4 anchovy fillets, finely chopped
100 ml (3½ fl oz) extra virgin olive oil
½ teaspoon Dijon mustard
1 lemon, juiced

METHOD

- Preheat oven to 200°C (400°F).
- Spread carrots and pumpkin wedges in a single layer across a large baking tray. Drizzle with 2 tablespoons of the oil, sprinkle with salt and using your hands, rub the vegetables so they're evenly coated. Roast in the oven for 25–30 minutes or until the vegetables are just soft but golden around the edges.
- Place kale in a bowl and toss with remaining 1 tablespoon of olive oil. Set aside until the pumpkin and carrots have cooked.
- Remove the carrot and pumpkin from the oven and scatter the raw kale on top. Return to the oven for 7–9 minutes or until the kale is crisp.
- Meanwhile, make the pistou by combining all the ingredients together in a bowl and stir until combined. Alternatively, place all the pistou ingredients in a food processor and blend to combine. Season to taste.
- Remove the vegetables from the oven and transfer to large serving bowl or individual serving bowls. Scatter with pistou and serve immediately.

Note: Pistou is like a pesto but without the nuts and cheese, leave out the anchovy to make this vegetarian and vegan.

CARAMELIZED BEETROOT AND ZUCCHINI SALAD WITH SUMAC YOGURT

I love the sweet tanginess that sumac brings to this salad. It isn't as easy to source as other spices but it is worth adding to your spice collection—it is fabulous scattered over a lamb roast or sprinkled over dips like hummus.

INGREDIENTS

Roasted vegetables

600 g (1 lb 5 oz) beetroot, peeled and
   sliced into even wedges

3 large zucchini (courgette) sliced into
   3 cm (1¼ in) batons

1 teaspoon ground cumin

1 teaspoon ground cinnamon

2 tablespoons extra virgin olive oil

sea salt and freshly ground black pepper

Sumac yogurt

125 g (4½ oz) natural Greek yogurt

½ lemon, juiced

1 teaspoon sumac

1 garlic clove, finely grated

Salad

1 spring onion (scallion), thinly sliced

2 sprigs dill, chopped

100 g (3½ oz) baby rocket (arugula)

METHOD

- Preheat oven to 200°C (400°F).
- Spread beetroot wedges and zucchini batons, in a single layer, on a lined roasting tray (or two). Toss with cumin, cinnamon, oil and a pinch of salt and pepper. Roast for 35–40 minutes or until caramelized on the edges, tossing occasionally.
- While the vegetables are roasting, place yogurt, lemon juice, sumac and garlic in a bowl and stir to combine. Taste and season.
- Allow roasted vegetables to cool slightly. Place in a bowl together with spring onion, dill and rocket. Add dressing and toss to combine.
- Transfer to a serving bowl or individual bowls. Sprinkle with extra sumac, to serve.

CARAMELIZED ONIONS
WITH SOFT BOILED EGGS AND CHIMICHURRI

I'll admit, this is a slightly unusual mix of ingredients but trust me, it works. The soft-boiled eggs, sweet caramelized onions and the punchy Argentinian sauce, chimichurri, work harmoniously. I sometimes add a dollop of harissa-spiked mayo (3 tablespoons of mayo + 2 teaspoons harissa) to add some creaminess.

INGREDIENTS

2 tablespoons extra virgin olive oil

2 large brown onions, peeled and thinly sliced

6–8 free range eggs, at room temperature

3 tablespoons pine nuts

150 g (5¼ oz) baby rocket (arugula)

150 g (5¼ oz) cherry tomatoes

1 ripe avocado, peeled, de-stoned and thinly sliced

100 g (3½ oz) Chimichurri (p. 179)

METHOD

- To caramelize the onions, heat oil in a large frying pan to a medium-low temperature. Add onions and sauté, stirring regularly, until golden and caramelized, about 20 minutes. Set aside to cool.
- Meanwhile, place water and a generous pinch of sea salt in a large saucepan and bring to the boil. Gently submerge eggs and cook for exactly 6 minutes. Drain and run under cold water (if you prefer hard-boiled eggs, cook for 7–8 minutes). Once cool enough to handle, remove shell and slice in half lengthways.
- In a small frying pan, dry roast the pine nuts for 2 minutes or until lightly golden (watch closely as pine nuts burn quickly). Set aside until ready to assemble.
- Place rocket in a large bowl, add cherry tomatoes, avocado, caramelized onion and pour over half the chimichurri. Gently toss to combine.
- Divide the salad between bowls, top with eggs, scatter with toasted pine nuts and drizzle with remaining chimichurri.

Note: Don't worry if you've undercooked the eggs a little. I love it when the yolk oozes into the dressing, adding a rich creaminess to the salad.

BAKED GREEN FALAFEL WITH ROASTED CAPSICUM CHUTNEY AND ISRAELI CHOPPED SALAD

I find that everyone is quite particular about what makes the best falafel—some like theirs dense with a fried crust, others prefer a lighter filling but for me, I'm all about the herb-packed falafel. I've swapped the usual tahini yoghurt sauce with a sweet roasted capsicum chutney and instead of the Israeli Chopped Salad, this is also delicious with the Roasted Cherry Tomato and Eggplant Tabbouleh (p. 94).

INGREDIENTS

Roasted capsicum chutney
2 red capsicums (bell peppers), about 300 g (10½ oz), deseeded and cut into 5 cm (2 in) pieces
1 tablespoon olive oil
1 garlic clove
2 teaspoons apple cider vinegar
Sea salt and freshly ground black pepper

Baked green falafel
½ onion, finely chopped
3 garlic cloves, chopped
3 teaspoons sesame seeds
2 tablespoons olive oil
1 teaspoon ground cumin
½ teaspoon ground coriander
¼ teaspoon freshly ground black pepper
¼ teaspoon cayenne pepper (optional)
1 teaspoon sea salt
1 bunch flat leaf parsley, finely chopped
1 bunch coriander (cilantro), finely chopped
1 X 400 g (14 oz) tin chickpeas, drained and rinsed
Israeli Chopped Salad (p. 99), to serve

METHOD

- Preheat oven to 200°C (400°F).
- For the chutney, place capsicum pieces on a baking tray and toss with olive oil. Roast in the oven, tossing occasionally, for 35-40 minutes or until soft. Pour capsicum, making sure you scrape in all the juices and caramelised bits in the pan, into a food processor, together with the garlic and vinegar. Process until it reaches a chutney consistency (I prefer mine quite chunky but you can puree, if you prefer). Taste and season as necessary. Set aside.
- To make the falafel, place onion and garlic in a food processor and pulse until combined. Add remaining falafel ingredients and pulse until fully combined; scraping down the sides as necessary.
- Line a roasting tray with baking (parchment) paper. Scoop a tablespoon of mixture onto the tray, to form 12 discs or balls. The mixture may not hold together very well but don't worry, once the falafels are baked and cooled, they hold together.
- Transfer to the oven and roast until golden, about 18 minutes. Using a spatula, flip falafel over and continue to bake for a further 5 minutes or until golden on all sides.
- Divide Israeli chopped salad between bowls and top with falafel and a dollop of roasted capsicum chutney.

Note: If you're short of time, you can buy roasted capsicum in a jar however you may need to add a teaspoon or two of maple syrup as they tend to have a more vinegary, astringent taste. To keep this dish Dairy Free and Vegan, leave out the goat's cheese in the Israeli Chopped Salad.

GREEN PEA AND CAULIFLOWER FRITTERS WITH PAN-FRIED HALOUMI AND SAUCE VIERGE

Sauce vierge, which literally translates as 'virgin sauce' in French, is one of my Mum's (many) specialties. If you want, swap Sicilian olives for black kalamata olives. Rather than throwing your olive pits away, pop them into your olive oil jar to make infused oil—the pits impart a beautiful fruitiness.

INGREDIENTS

2 tablespoons extra virgin olive oil

250 g (9 oz) haloumi, cut into 1 cm (½ in) slices

250 g (9 oz) Twice Cooked Crunchy Garlic Quinoa (p. 192)

50 g (1¾ oz) mixed salad greens, to serve

Fritters

½ small cauliflower, about 300 g (10 ½ oz), broken into florets

300 g (10 ½ oz) fresh or frozen peas, podded and/or thawed

½ small onion, diced

3 free range eggs, gently whisked

½ teaspoon sea salt

½ teaspoon freshly ground black pepper

Sauce vierge

3 ripe plum tomatoes, skinned, deseeded and finely diced

2 garlic cloves, finely chopped

50 g (1¾ oz) green Sicilian olives, pitted and finely chopped

1 teaspoon chives, finely chopped

1 teaspoon tarragon, finely chopped

1 teaspoon basil leaves, finely chopped

1 lemon, juiced

1 tablespoon extra virgin olive oil

sea salt and freshly ground pepper

METHOD

- To make the fritters, bring a medium saucepan of water to a simmer. Add cauliflower florets and cook until tender, about 15 minutes. Drain in a colander and allow to cool. Remove any excess water with a kitchen towel or absorbent paper.
- Place cooled cauliflower, 200 g (7 oz) of the peas, onion and eggs in a food processor. Blend to a purée and then stir through remaining 100 g (3½ oz) of peas to create a thick batter.
- Meanwhile, prepare the sauce vierge by combining all the ingredients in a small bowl. Season to taste.
- Heat half the oil (1 tablespoon) in a large frying pan to a medium-high temperature. Once the pan is hot, spoon in a dollop of the cauliflower batter for each fritter. Do not overcrowd the pan and you don't want the fritters to be too thin. Carefully flip each fritter (they can be quite delicate) and cook until both sides are lightly golden around the edges. Repeat with remaining fritters.
- In a separate frying pan, heat the remaining 1 tablespoon of olive oil. Add haloumi and cook for 2 minutes on each side or until golden.
- Divide Twice Cooked Crunchy Garlic Quinoa between bowls, top with salad greens and serve fritters with sauce vierge and haloumi.

Note: Salad greens can include baby spinach, rocket, curly endive and mizuna (a type of lettuce). To make this vegetarian, use vegetable broth when making the Twice Cooked Crunchy Garlic Quinoa (p. 192).

Let's Eat Meat

Much of my love for real, whole foods stems from growing up on a sheep and cattle farm in rural Australia. As a child, I didn't think it was unusual to be eating everything homemade—from bread and stews to cakes, jams and relishes—and of course, enjoying our own meat. It is only later in life that I've come to realise how fortunate this upbringing was. It is also this connection to the land that has shaped my passion for cooking and food.

Healthy eating is often viewed as being synonymous with restrictive eating however I believe a whole foods diet encourages moderation and a holistic approach to your health and wellbeing. There was a time when I avoided red meat, however, now I choose quality meat, over quantity. For me, the health of the animal is important to the quality of the meat. I buy organic and free range as often as possible and this is something that I recommend, if possible.

The Fiery Kung Pao Chicken (p. 119) is a favorite in our household when we're craving something spicy and flavor packed. I'm a lover of cooking with skewers, especially for summer barbecues and picnics. Without a doubt, my two favorites are the Smoky Spiced Beef Skewers with Tandoori Cashew Sauce (p. 120) and Peanut Butter Chicken Skewers with Quick Bean Salad (p. 123). As the days grow dark and cold, I dream of bowls of the Spicy Dan Dan Noodles with Pork and Chili Oil (p. 126).

CUBAN MOJO CHICKEN BOWL WITH ROASTED RADISHES, CAULIFLOWER COUS COUS AND CITRUS ALMOND DRESSING

My good friends Alex and Nick recently went to Cuba and in lieu of going myself, I became obsessed with researching the cuisine (does anyone else do that?). In Cuban cooking, mojo applies to any sauce that is made with garlic, olive oil and orange juice—here it doubles as the marinade for the chicken and the dressing for the dish.

INGREDIENTS

Mojo Marinade
1 teaspoon orange zest

3 tablespoons fresh orange juice

3 tablespoons fresh lime juice

2 tablespoons fresh oregano, finely chopped

3 garlic cloves, finely chopped

2 small pickled jalapeños, finely chopped

1 teaspoon sea salt

2 tablespoons extra virgin olive oil

2 large free range chicken breasts (about 600 g/1 lb 5 oz)

Cuban bowl
4 red or yellow baby beetroots, peeled and quartered

1 bunch radishes, halved

2 tablespoons extra virgin olive oil

sea salt and freshly ground black pepper, to taste

2 tablespoons Quick Garlicky Hummus (p. 185) or store-bought (optional)

150 g (5¼ oz) store-bought marinated artichokes in a jar, drained

METHOD

- Preheat oven to 200°C (400°F).
- To make the mojo marinade, combine all the ingredients in a medium bowl and whisk until combined. Reserve half the marinade for the citrus almond dressing. Place remaining mojo marinade in a bowl and add chicken. Cover and marinate for as long as possible, preferably overnight.
- Place the beetroot and radishes on a lined baking tray and toss with olive oil, sea salt and pepper. Place chicken on the same tray (if your tray is large enough, otherwise use a separate tray) and roast in the oven for 15 minutes. After 15 minutes, remove the chicken from the oven and set aside to rest. Give the veggies a toss and roast for a further 5–10 minutes or until the beetroot is golden around the edges.
- Meanwhile, to make the cous cous (p. 116), place the cauliflower in a food processor and pulse in 10 second increments (to avoid turning the cauliflower to mush) until the texture resembles the texture of cous cous or rice (if you don't have a food processor, you can make this by simply grating the cauliflower on a box grater—it is a little more time consuming but gets the job done.)
- Heat oil or butter in a large frying pan to a medium temperature and add the cauliflower cous cous. Stirring occasionally, cook until the oil or butter has coated all the cauliflower and it is warm, about 5–10 minutes.
- For the citrus almond dressing, place the remaining half of the mojo sauce in a bowl. Add the almond butter and coriander and stir to combine. Season to taste and add a few tablespoons of warm water until you reach a thick but pourable consistency.
- To assemble, divide the cauliflower cous cous between the bowls. Slice

continues next page

CUBAN MOJO CHICKEN BOWL WITH ROASTED RADISHES, CAULIFLOWER COUS COUS AND CITRUS ALMOND DRESSING

1–2 ripe avocados, peeled, de-stoned
  and thinly sliced
handful of mixed dry roasted nuts
baby herbs, to serve (optional)

Cauliflower cous cous
1 cauliflower (about 700 g/1 lb 7 oz),
  broken into florets
1 tablespoon butter or extra virgin olive
  oil (for dairy free)

Citrus almond dressing
3 tablespoons Roasted Almond Butter
  (p. 181) or any nut butter
½ bunch fresh coriander (cilantro)
sea salt, to taste

the chicken and divide between bowls together with beetroot, radishes, hummus, artichokes and sliced avocado. Drizzle with citrus almond dressing, allowing it to seep through to the cauliflower cous cous. Scatter with mixed nuts and baby herbs.

Note: To make this paleo friendly, skip the hummus.

GREEK LAMB SOUVLAKI WITH BEETROOT TZATZIKI AND QUICK PICKLED CUCUMBER SALAD

Souvlaki, meaning skewers in Greek, is traditionally made with pork however I'm drawn to the richness of lamb, which I think works beautifully with this simple Mediterranean dish. Soaking your skewers overnight prevents them from burning.

INGREDIENTS

1 teaspoon lemon zest
3 tablespoons lemon juice
3 tablespoons olive oil
4 garlic cloves, finely chopped
2 tablespoons fresh oregano, finely chopped
1 tablespoon fresh rosemary, finely chopped
1 teaspoon sea salt
½ teaspoon freshly ground black pepper
750 g (1 lb 10 oz) lamb (leg or shoulder), cut into 3 cm (1¼ in) cubes
8 long wooden skewers, soaked overnight
Roasted Mixed Potatoes (p. 157), to serve
Beetroot Tzatziki (p. 186), to serve

Quick pickled cucumber salad
4 Lebanese cucumbers, thinly sliced
¼ Spanish onion, thinly sliced
1 teaspoon sea salt
2 tablespoons dill, roughly chopped
1 tablespoon red wine vinegar

METHOD

- In a large bow, combine lemon zest, juice, olive oil, garlic, oregano, rosemary, salt and pepper. Add lamb cubes and toss to combine. Cover and refrigerate for at least 3 hours or preferably overnight.
- Meanwhile, to make the salad, place cucumbers and Spanish onion in a bowl and sprinkle with sea salt. Using your hands, mix until the cucumbers begin to soften and release liquid. Set aside for 20 minutes or up to 2 hours. Drain off liquid and lightly squeeze the cucumbers and onion. Place in a serving bowl and add dill and vinegar.
- When ready to cook, preheat a grill pan or barbecue to high. Thread lamb onto pre-soaked skewers. When the pan is hot, cook skewers (in batches if necessary), turning occasionally, for 5–8 minutes or until cooked through.
- Allow the skewers to rest for 5 minutes before serving.
- Divide mixed roasted potatoes between bowls, top with skewers, a dollop of beetroot tzatziki and quick pickled cucumber salad.

Note: To make this dairy free and paleo, skip the beetroot tzatziki.

CHICKEN LEGS, HONEY AND LEMON BAKE WITH GARLIC SAUCE

An easy and inexpensive way to feed a crowd, this dish takes barely a moment to pull together. The sweetness of the honey, coupled with a good dose of tart lemon creates something special with little effort on your part.

INGREDIENTS

2 lemons, juiced

1 tablespoon extra virgin olive oil

3 tablespoons honey

large handful of walnuts

2 garlic cloves, finely chopped

sea salt and freshly ground pepper

8 free range chicken drumsticks
    (1½ kg / 3 lb), skin on

1 lemon, cut into 8 wedges

Garlic sauce

4 garlic cloves, finely chopped

sea salt

100 ml (3½ fl oz) extra virgin olive oil

METHOD

- Preheat oven to 200°C (400°F).
- Place the lemon juice in a large bowl. Add olive oil, honey, walnuts and garlic and stir to combine. Add chicken drumsticks and leave to marinate for at least 15 minutes or overnight, if possible.
- When ready to cook, lay the chicken drumsticks on a roasting tray lined with baking (parchment) paper, basting with the marinade. Tuck the lemon wedges around the chicken drumsticks.
- Roast for 35–40 minutes, turning occasionally, or until the chicken is cooked.
- Meanwhile, make the garlic sauce. Place garlic in a mortar, season with salt and pound to a very fine paste using the pestle. Transfer garlic paste to a small bowl and gradually whisk in oil until it thickens.
- Divide chicken between bowls and drizzle with garlic sauce.

Note: For a more substantial meal, serve with the Roasted Pumpkin, Quinoa, Chia and Mustard Vinaigrette Nourishing Bowl (p. 76) or for a paleo option, serve alongside roasted sweet potato wedges.

FIERY KUNG PAO CHICKEN
WITH TWICE COOKED CRUNCHY GARLIC QUINOA

I was first introduced to Kung Pao chicken, a classic Chinese dish from the Szechuan province, on a trip to New York City with one of my best friends, Nat. I've been hooked on this spicy, slightly sweet stir fry ever since. This is my healthy twist.

INGREDIENTS

6 dried long red chilies, deseeded and coarsely chopped

2 tablespoons coconut oil

1 onion, sliced lengthways

½ red capsicum (bell pepper), sliced into 3 cm (1¼ in) long and 1 cm (½ in) wide strips

4 garlic cloves, finely chopped

2 teaspoons ginger, finely grated

2 teaspoons Sichuan peppercorns

750 g (1 lb 10 oz) free range chicken breast (or thigh fillets), cut into 2.5 cm (1 in) pieces

125 ml Chicken Broth (p. 187)

3 tablespoons dry sherry

2 tablespoons tamari (or light soy sauce)

1 teaspoon sesame oil

4 spring onions (scallions), cut into 2.5 cm (1 in) pieces

3 tablespoons roasted peanuts, roughly chopped

METHOD

- Add chopped dried chilies to a large wok and heat to a medium-high temperature. Dry roast for about 1 minute or until fragrant. Remove from wok and set aside.
- Using the same wok, heat half the oil (1 tablespoon) to a medium-high temperature. Add the onions and capsicum and stir-fry until onion is translucent and capsicum is golden at the edges. Add garlic and ginger and cook until lightly golden, about 2 minutes. Remove from wok and set aside.
- Coarsely crush Sichuan peppercorns in a mortar and pestle. Heat the remaining oil in the wok to a medium temperature and add the Sichuan peppercorns. Stir-fry until fragrant, about 1 minute.
- Add chicken, in batches, and stir-fry until chicken is cooked and golden brown (3–4 minutes).
- Return all the chicken to the wok, together with the roasted dried chili and sautéed onion, capsicum, garlic and ginger. Turn up the heat to the highest temperature and stir in the broth, sherry, tamari, sesame oil, spring onions and peanuts. Toss to combine and serve immediately with your choice of grain.

Note: I love serving this with either the Rainbow Ginger Fried Wild Rice (p. 82) or Twice Cooked Crunchy Garlic Quinoa (p. 192).

SMOKY SPICED BEEF SKEWERS
WITH TANDOORI CASHEW SAUCE

This is what I would describe as a stalwart recipe. It never fails to impress whether for a casual barbecue or a sit-down dinner. Marinating the steak in yogurt and lemon tenderizes the meat, especially if you can leave it overnight.

INGREDIENTS

200 g (7 oz) natural Greek yogurt, unsweetened
3 garlic cloves, finely chopped
2 teaspoons smoked paprika
1 teaspoon ground cumin
½ teaspoon ground turmeric
½ teaspoon ground cinnamon
¼ teaspoon chili powder
2 tablespoons lemon juice
2 tablespoons extra virgin olive oil
750 g (1 lb 10 oz) rump steak, thinly sliced
Rainbow Ginger Fried Wild Rice (p. 82), to serve
few sprigs of coriander (cilantro)
few sprigs of mint

Tandoori cashew sauce
100 g (3½ oz) roasted cashews, unsalted
1 garlic clove, roughly chopped
1 teaspoon fresh ginger, finely grated
125 ml (4 fl oz) coconut milk
2 teaspoons honey
2 teaspoons Tandoori Spice Mix (p. 189) or store-bought paste

METHOD

- In a large bowl, combine the Greek yogurt, garlic, paprika, cumin, turmeric, cinnamon, chili powder, lemon juice and olive oil. Add the rump steak, toss to coat, cover and place in the refrigerator for 3 hours or overnight.
- Meanwhile, place the cashews in a high-powered stick blender or food processor. Process until the cashews break down and it forms a smooth paste (a similar consistency to smooth peanut butter), up to 4—5 minutes. Then add garlic, ginger, coconut milk, honey and tandoori spice mix (if using store-bought paste, add half the amount to start and taste before adding more). Blend until it reaches a creamy sauce. Season to taste and set aside until ready to serve.
- Remove the marinated steak from the refrigerator an hour before cooking to bring to room temperature.
- When ready to cook, preheat a grill pan or barbecue to high.
- Thread the marinated beef onto skewers, leaving a little space between the meat to maximize crispy bits. Reserve leftover marinade to baste. Cook the skewers, 2—3 minutes per side, using a basting brush to coat with reserved marinade. Remove from the heat.
- To serve, divide the rainbow ginger fried wild rice between bowls, top with beef skewers, warmed tandoori cashew sauce and scatter with coriander and mint.

FOOLPROOF OVEN-BAKED SESAME CHICKEN THIGHS WITH BUTTER BEAN MASH

Allowing the chicken to marinate overnight will give the dish an extra oomph of flavor. If the butter bean mash isn't your thing, you could also rustle up some steamed rice. I prefer to use chicken thighs with their bone in but you can easily use thighs sans bone.

INGREDIENTS

8 garlic cloves, finely chopped
1 teaspoon ginger, finely grated
2 small chilies, seeds in, thinly sliced
3 tablespoons honey
3 tablespoons tamari (or light soy sauce)
2 tablespoons apple cider vinegar
1 teaspoon sesame oil
4 free range chicken thighs, bone-in and
    skin on (about 900 g/2 lb)
2 teaspoons sesame seeds, toasted
1 lemon, sliced into wedges

Butter bean mash

2 tablespoons extra virgin olive oil
2 garlic cloves, finely chopped
2 x 400 g (14 oz) butter beans, rinsed
    and drained
150 ml (5 fl oz) Chicken Broth (p. 187)
    or water
sea salt and freshly ground pepper

METHOD

- In a bowl, combine the garlic, ginger, chilies, honey, tamari, apple cider vinegar and sesame oil. Place marinade and chicken in a large resealable plastic bag or container. Turn to coat and marinate for at least 12 hours..
- Preheat oven to 200°C (400°F).
- Place the chicken, skin side up, in an oven-safe baking dish. Bake, turning and basting with the marinade halfway through, until the thighs are brown and cooked through, about 30–35 minutes. Remove from oven and set aside to rest for 5 minutes.
- Meanwhile, make the butter bean mash. Heat oil in large frying pan over a medium temperature and add garlic. Sauté until lightly golden. Add butter beans and broth and simmer, uncovered, until heated through, about 5 minutes. Remove from heat and, using a potato masher, crush to a creamy consistency or blend in a food processor. Season to taste.
- To serve, divide mash between bowls, top with chicken, scatter with toasted sesame seeds and serve with lemon wedges.

PEANUT BUTTER CHICKEN SKEWERS WITH QUICK BEAN SALAD

I'm always on the hunt for recipes that can be done ahead of time and dishes that can easily be transported to picnics and barbecues—this one fits the bill. I used to have this bean salad for lunch all the time and it shocked me the number of people who asked for the recipe. If you're feeding the little ones, skip the chili powder and they'll devour this too.

INGREDIENTS

750 g (1 lb 10 oz) skinless free range chicken thighs, deboned and cut into 3 cm (1¼ in) pieces

Marinade
1 tablespoon extra virgin olive oil
2 garlic cloves, finely chopped
1 teaspoon ground cumin
1 teaspoon garam masala
½ teaspoon ground cinnamon
½ teaspoon chili powder (optional)
½ teaspoon sea salt
3 tablespoons crunchy peanut butter
125 ml (4 fl oz) coconut cream

Bean salad
300 g (10½ oz) green beans, topped, tailed and chopped into 3 cm (1¼ in) batons
¼ brown onion, peeled and finely diced
½ red capsicum (bell pepper), seeds removed and finely diced
1 x 420 g (15 oz) tin four bean mix, washed and drained

Dressing
80 ml (2¾ fl oz) white vinegar
3 tablespoons extra virgin olive oil
1 tablespoon caster (superfine) sugar
1 teaspoon sea salt
½ teaspoon ground pepper

METHOD

- Combine all of the marinade ingredients in a bowl and add chicken pieces, tossing to coat. Cover and refrigerate for at least 3 hours or overnight.
- Meanwhile, to start the bean salad, bring a large pot of salted water to the boil. Add green beans and cook until al dente, about 4 minutes. Drain and place in a bowl (beans still hot) with onion and capsicum—the heat softens the onion and capsicum slightly.
- To prepare the dressing, place vinegar, oil, sugar, salt and pepper in a small saucepan and heat until sugar has dissolved. Pour warm dressing over green bean mix. Cover with plastic wrap and leave for 10 minutes to allow the flavors to develop. Stir through the four bean mix and leave for a further few minutes.
- When ready to cook, thread chicken onto skewers that have been presoaked in cold water. Heat the remaining oil (1 tablespoon) in a char-grill pan or barbecue to a medium–high temperature. Working in batches, cook chicken skewers, turning occasionally, for 8 minutes or until cooked through.
- Allow the skewers to rest for 5 minutes before serving with bean salad.

Note: Dark-meat chicken (such as thighs) is the best for grilling as it doesn't tend to dry out. The bean salad is best eaten the day after so it makes a great dish to take to barbecues. Substitute four bean mix with the same amount of assorted beans such as chickpeas, butter beans, red kidney beans.

INDONESIAN-STYLE BEEF GADO GADO

True to its name, Gado Gado, which means 'potpourri', is a colorful array of blanched vegetables, generously doused in an aromatic and creamy peanut sauce. It's typically served with fried tofu and hard-boiled eggs however I love the addition of the just-seared steak.

INGREDIENTS

Peanut sauce

1 teaspoon shrimp paste

140 g (5 oz) crunchy peanut butter (no added sugar)

125 ml (4 fl oz) coconut milk

2 garlic cloves, roughly chopped

1 long red chili, deseeded and finely chopped

1 tablespoon lime juice

80 ml (2¾ fl oz) water, to thin sauce

Gado Gado

3 tablespoons extra virgin olive oil

200 g (7 oz) firm tofu, drained, pressed, and cut into 2 cm (¾ in) thick triangles

200 g (7 oz) Chinese cabbage (wombok), tough stems trimmed, roughly chopped

100 g (3½ oz) long beans or regular green beans, trimmed and cut into bite size batons, about 5 cm (2 in)

100 g (3½ oz) bean sprouts

2 medium carrots, sliced ½ cm (¼ in) on an angle

1 Lebanese cucumber, sliced ½ cm (¼ in) thick on an angle

2 eggs, hard-boiled, peeled and halved

2 x 250–300 g (9–10½ oz) scotch fillet steaks

sea salt and freshly ground pepper

METHOD

- Place shrimp paste in a small saucepan and heat over a medium-low temperature. Stirring constantly to break down the paste, cook until the mixture becomes dry and slightly crumbly. Add peanut butter, coconut milk, garlic, chili and lime juice and cook, stirring constantly for 2–3 minutes. Set aside to cool slightly.
- In a large non-stick frying pan, heat half (1½ tablespoons) of the oil over a medium temperature and fry tofu until golden and crunchy, about 2 minutes on each side. Drain tofu on absorbent paper and set aside until ready to serve.
- Bring a large saucepan of salted water to the boil. Working in batches, cook cabbage, beans, sprouts and carrots until just tender (2–3 minutes for carrots, 30 seconds to 1 minute for cabbage, beans and sprouts). Using a slotted spoon, transfer vegetables to a bowl of ice water to chill completely. Drain vegetables, spread on absorbent paper or a kitchen towel to dry and transfer to a large platter.
- Heat a barbecue or char-grill pan to a high temperature, brush beef with remaining (1½ tablespoons) of oil and season with sea salt and freshly ground black pepper. Cook for 3–5 minutes on each side for medium–rare. Rest for 5 minutes.
- Reheat the peanut sauce in a small saucepan and add water gradually to thin the consistency. Use only enough water to reach a pouring consistency (you may need less or more).
- Thinly slice the beef. Arrange the vegetables in bowls and then the beef. Top with crunchy tofu, eggs and drizzle generously with peanut sauce.

SPICY DAN DAN NOODLES WITH PORK AND CHILI OIL

This typical Sichuan dish is a must for anyone who appreciates a good kick of chili. Using flat rice noodles may not be authentic for dan dan but it tastes delicious—feel free to use fresh egg noodles if you can get your hands on them.

INGREDIENTS

Chili oil

2 teaspoons Sichuan peppercorns,
   crushed

2 teaspoons chili flakes, crushed

3 tablespoons extra virgin olive oil

Dan dan noodles

300 g (10½ oz) dried flat rice noodles
   (Shanghai-style noodles or udon, if
   not gluten intolerant)

1 tablespoon rice bran oil (or vegetable)

600 g (1 lb 5 oz) pork mince

1 teaspoon ginger, finely grated

180 ml (6 fl oz) Chicken Broth (p. 187)
   or any stock/broth of choice

2 tablespoons red wine vinegar

2 tablespoons tamari (or light soy sauce)

1 tablespoon tahini (sesame seed paste
   or even crunchy peanut butter)

1 teaspoon Sichuan peppercorns,
   crushed

3 spring onions (scallions), thinly sliced

1 lime, cut into wedges

METHOD

- Begin by making your chili oil. In a small saucepan, add the Sichuan peppercorns, chili flakes and oil. Over low heat, simmer for a few minutes or until fragrant, and then turn off. Set aside and allow the oil to cool.
- Meanwhile, cook noodles in a large pot of boiling water until just tender but still firm to the bite (al dente). Drain well and divide between bowls.
- Heat oil in a medium frying pan or wok to a medium temperature. Add pork and ginger and stir, breaking up pork with a spatula, until cooked through and lightly browned. Stir in chicken broth, red wine vinegar, tamari, tahini and Sichuan peppercorns; simmer until sauce thickens, about 7 minutes.
- Pour pork mixture over noodles, scatter with spring onions and drizzle with chili oil. Serve with lime wedges.

HERB AND CHILI TURKEY MINCE
WITH ZUCCHINI NOODLES AND FRIED EGG

Holy smokes, I really love zucchini noodles. I'd seen them in recipes and on Instagram long before I dared try them (I mean, how good could zucchinis grated into noodles really be?) and it really did surprise me how much I enjoyed them—now I'm on Team Zoodle. This is a recipe for days when you want something effortlessly satisfying yet still light and fresh.

INGREDIENTS

6 teaspoons coconut oil (or any neutral oil)

4–6 medium zucchini (courgette), about 500 g (1 lb)

2 free range eggs

Stir-fried turkey mince

½ onion, peeled and diced

2 garlic cloves, finely chopped

1 teaspoon ginger, grated

1 large chili, deseed and chopped

250 g (9 oz) lean turkey (or free range chicken) mince

2 teaspoons tamari (or light soy sauce)

2 teaspoons gluten free fish sauce

1 teaspoon sambal oelek or chili paste, plus more, to serve

½ teaspoon untoasted sesame oil

½ lime, juiced

1 tablespoon fresh coriander (cilantro), roughly chopped

1 tablespoon fresh basil, roughly chopped

METHOD

• Cut zucchinis into noodle strips using a spiralizer, mandolin or good knife skills.

• Heat 2 teaspoons of the coconut oil in a large non-stick frying pan over a high temperature. Add zucchini noodles and cook, stirring occasionally, for 7–8 minutes or until lightly golden but still firm (not mushy). You may need to add more coconut oil, depending on the size of your frying pan.

• Heat another 2 teaspoons of oil and fry eggs, cooking only until the whites are set but the yolk is still runny.

• Heat the remaining oil (2 teaspoons) in the same wok or frying pan over medium-high heat. Add the onion and sauté for 2–3 minutes or until translucent. Stir in garlic, ginger and chili and cook for a further 2–3 minutes. Add turkey and cook until the meat has browned. Stir through tamari, fish sauce, sambal oelek, sesame oil and lime. Toss to combine. Add coriander and basil.

• Divide zucchini 'noodles' between bowls, top with stir-fried turkey and fried egg and drizzle with extra chili paste, if desired.

GRILLED LAMB TIKKA WITH CARAMELIZED NECTARINES AND PINE NUT AND PISTACHIO RAITA

I like to serve this dish for a Sunday lunch with little bowls of each component set out on the table—allowing guests to help themselves. The caramelized nectarines are up for discussion—if you're the kind of person who likes fruit in savoury dishes, this will be right up your alley but it works just as well without.

INGREDIENTS

Lamb tikka
1 tablespoon Tandoori Spice Mix
  (p. 189) or store-bought paste
3 tablespoons natural Greek yogurt
2 teaspoons sesame oil
2 x 250 g (9 oz) lamb backstraps or
  fillets
extra virgin olive oil, for grilling
Twice Cooked Crunchy Garlic Quinoa
  (p. 192), to serve

Pine nut and pistachio raita
2 tablespoons pine nuts
2 tablespoons pistachios
250 g (9 oz) natural Greek yogurt
2 teaspoons lemon juice
2 tablespoons mint, roughly chopped

Caramelized nectarines
2 ripe, firm yellow (or white)
  nectarines (or peaches), halved
1 tablespoon balsamic vinegar

METHOD

- Combine tandoori spice mix, yogurt and sesame oil in a large bowl. (If using store-bought paste, omit sesame oil). Add lamb and toss to coat. Marinate for at least 30 minutes (preferably overnight).
- Dry roast pine nuts and pistachios in a frying pan over low heat. Stir constantly (as pine nuts can burn quickly) and remove from heat as soon as the pine nuts are lightly golden. Roughly chop and place in a bowl with Greek yogurt, lemon juice and mint. Set aside until ready to serve.
- In a bowl, toss together the nectarines and balsamic vinegar.
- Preheat the barbecue, grill or a grill pan to a high temperature. Place the lamb on the barbecue or grill and cook about 5 minutes per side (cooking time will vary depending on the thickness of your lamb). Once grilled on both sides, remove, cover with foil and allow to rest for 5 minutes.
- Grill nectarines, cut side down first until they begin to caramelize and grill marks begin to appear. Flip and lightly grill the other side, about 30 seconds.
- To serve, divide Twice Cooked Crunchy Garlic Quinoa between bowls. Slice lamb and place on top with raita and caramelized nectarines.

Note: If you can tolerate gluten, serve with store-bought warmed garlic naan bread.

Fancy Festive *Food*

This chapter is about celebrating those moments when we share a meal with others, whether it be at Christmas, birthdays or any celebration or impromptu get-together.

Don't be put off by the title of this chapter—I don't do elaborate, fiddly food. I never, ever want to be fussing over a dish at the last minute. I serve dishes that can be prepared ahead of time and I never serve individual plates in that awkward, restaurant-style-at-home sort of way. Here are some simple ideas for special occasions.

CLASSIC SUMMER FEAST

- Crab, chili and avocado lettuce boats (p. 38)
- Crunchy cauliflower salad with mango, lime and jalapeño dressing (p. 100)
- Stuffed turkey with quinoa, cranberry and pistachio (p. 143)
- Pavlova parfaits with coconut lime cream, banana, kiwifruit and passionfruit (p. 168)

AN ITALIAN-INSPIRED CHRISTMAS

- Parmesan, ricotta and Gruyère sweet potato arancini balls with basil mayonnaise (p. 35)
- Christmas pork shoulder with chili and fennel (p. 134)
- Smashed baby potatoes with prosciutto crackling and dill sour cream dressing (p. 148)
- Shaved fennel and crushed macadamia salad with confit garlic dressing (p. 97)
- Simple strawberry and balsamic semifreddo (p. 161)

MIDDLE EASTERN FEAST

- Whole roasted spiced cauliflower with tahini yogurt dressing (p. 96)
- Roasted cherry tomato and eggplant tabbouleh with garlicky hummus dressing (p. 94)
- Sticky pomegranate chicken with Iranian jewelled rice (p. 141)
- Sumac lamb chops with buckwheat, crumbled feta and pomegranate (p. 133)
- Flourless carrot and pineapple cake with lemon thyme syrup and labneh (p. 173)

ASIAN TAPAS

- Salmon san choy bao (p. 36)
- Marinated mushrooms with garlic, chili and white balsamic vinegar (p. 39)
- Sticky tamarind, sesame and lime chicken wings (p. 42)
- Peking duck breast rice paper rolls with plum dipping sauce (p. 138)
- Cashew, date and caramel slice cups (p. 171)

SUMMER BARBECUE

- Harissa prawns with charred corn, sugar snap pea and beetroot slaw (p. 56)
- Herbed feta dip with farmers' market crudités (p. 46)
- Summer in a bowl with mango and herbed quinoa (p. 80)
- Barbecue carrots with tangy buttermilk and dill dressing (p. 155)
- Peach, white chocolate and macadamia tartlets (p. 170)

GIRLS' NIGHT IN

- Spiced quinoa and zucchini patties with avocado aioli (p. 83)
- Kaffir lime and chili seafood skewers with mango, cucumber and herb noodle salad (p. 52)
- All things green with sweet sesame sauce (p. 102)
- No-bake yogurt and mango cheesecake pots with cashew coconut crust (p. 174)

SUMAC LAMB CHOPS WITH BUCKWHEAT, CRUMBLED FETA AND POMEGRANATE

Just a modest scattering of sumac takes the humble lamb chop to the next level. This Middle Eastern inspired salad is a favorite, not just with these lamb chops but with any grilled meat or seafood. Pomegranate molasses is simply the concentrated juice of the pomegranate fruit. It's full of antioxidants, vitamins and minerals and adds a tangy Middle Eastern flair to dishes.

INGREDIENTS

2 teaspoons sumac
2 tablespoons extra virgin olive oil
8 lamb cutlets, French trimmed
sea salt and freshly ground black pepper

Buckwheat salad
200 g (7 oz) raw buckwheat, washed
  and rinsed
750 ml (1¼ pt) water
3 tablespoons extra virgin olive oil
2 tablespoons sherry vinegar (or red
  wine vinegar)
2 tablespoons pomegranate molasses
½ bunch mint, roughly chopped
½ bunch flat leaf parsley, roughly
  chopped
½ bunch dill fronds, roughly chopped
100 g (3½ oz) feta, crumbled
seeds (arils) from 1 pomegranate,
  to serve
handful of toasted buckwheat
  (optional), to serve

METHOD

- Place sumac and olive oil in a bowl. Add lamb and massage the oil mix into the meat. Allow to marinate for at least 15–20 minutes or preferably up to 2 hours.
- Place buckwheat and water in a saucepan and bring to the boil. Reduce heat, cover and cook until al dente, about 20–25 minutes. Set aside to cool.
- Whisk together olive oil, vinegar and pomegranate molasses in a large bowl. Add cooled buckwheat, herbs, feta and half the pomegranate arils. Toss to combine. Set aside.
- Heat a large char-grill pan or barbecue to a medium-high temperature and cook lamb, turning occasionally, until charred, about 8–10 minutes. Season, cover loosely with foil and set aside to rest, about 5 minutes.
- Divide salad between bowls, top with 2 lamb chops per person, scatter with remaining pomegranate arils. If you like, drizzle with a little extra pomegranate molasses and scatter with toasted buckwheat for extra crunch.

CHRISTMAS PORK SHOULDER WITH CHILI AND FENNEL

Growing up, our family could never agree on the Christmas menu, which inevitably meant we'd just make everything and have enough food to feed us for weeks thereafter (but that's Christmas, right?). I always requested turkey. My mum wanted fresh prawns (shrimp), Sam loved a fillet of beef, Dad craved the classic glazed ham while, according to my brother Hugh, it wouldn't have been Christmas without this pork shoulder—with crackling, of course.

INGREDIENTS

1 free range, bone-in pork shoulder, about 4–5 kg (8 lb 12 oz–11 lb)
2 tablespoons fennel seeds
1 tablespoon dried chili flakes
1 tablespoon sea salt
1 head garlic, cloves peeled
3 tablespoons extra virgin olive oil
Salsa Verde (p. 184), to serve

METHOD

- Preheat oven to 220°C (425°F).
- Carefully score the skin of the pork in a 2.5 cm (1 in) criss-cross pattern, just deep enough to penetrate the fat without exposing the flesh.
- In a mortar and pestle, pound fennel seeds, chili, salt and garlic to a paste. Using your hands, rub oil over the pork and then add the spices, pushing into the scored skin.
- Place pork, skin-side up, in a large, deep roasting pan. Roast for 30 minutes or until the skin of the pork has started to puff up and you can see it turning into crackling. At this point, turn the heat down to 170°C (325°F) and pop the pork back into the oven and roast for a further 4½–5 hours.
- Remove shoulder from the pan, cover and set aside to rest for 15–20 minutes.
- Serve with salsa verde.

Note: This is great served as part of a banquet with Roasted Mixed Potatoes (p. 157) and Shaved Fennel and Crushed Macadamia Salad with Confit Garlic Dressing (p. 97).

SHREDDED VIETNAMESE LAMB WITH RICE NOODLES AND NUOC CHAM

This is a reassuringly undemanding dish—pop it all in a pot and let the magic happen. The combination of Vietnamese flavors with lamb is slightly unconventional but works wonderfully well. Lamb shoulder is fattier than the leg and it becomes meltingly tender after a good braise. The herbs add a leafy freshness while the nuoc cham adds a tart sweetness.

INGREDIENTS

1 stalk lemongrass, bruised

2 garlic cloves, finely chopped

2 cm (¾ in) ginger, peeled and finely chopped

2 tablespoons rice vinegar

3 tablespoons gluten free fish sauce

1 tablespoon tamari (or light soy sauce)

3 coriander (cilantro) roots

3 L (5¼ pt) water

1.5 kg (3 lb) lamb shoulder, bone-in, trimmed

250 g (9 oz) dried rice noodles

¼ bunch coriander (cilantro), to serve

¼ bunch Vietnamese mint, to serve

100 g (3½ oz) bean sprouts, to serve

Nuoc cham

3 tablespoons white vinegar

3 tablespoons lime juice

2 tablespoons gluten free fish sauce

2 teaspoons honey

1 red birds eye chili, finely chopped

1 garlic clove, finely chopped

METHOD

- Place lemongrass, garlic, ginger, rice vinegar, fish sauce, tamari, coriander roots and water in a large saucepan or stockpot and bring to the boil. Add lamb, reduce heat to low, cover and simmer until the lamb is tender, about 2 to 2½ hours. Remove from heat, leaving the lamb to cool in the liquid. Remove and coarsely shred the meat, reserving the broth to pour over the noodles.
- Meanwhile, place the rice noodles in a medium bowl and cover completely with boiling water. Cover with plastic wrap and leave for 15–20 minutes or until softened. Drain noodles and rinse with cold water.
- For the nuoc cham, combine ingredients in a bowl and season to taste.
- To serve, arrange noodles in bowls, top with shredded lamb and spoon over reserved broth. Scatter with coriander, mint and bean sprouts and then drizzle with nuoc cham.

Note: Once you've shredded the meat, keep the lamb bone to make broth.

BUTTERFLIED ROASTED THAI RED CURRY SPATCHCOCK

For days when you crave the comfort of a good ol' roast chook but also the spiciness of bold, Thai flavors, this satiates both desires. I've included quantities to use store-bought curry paste but this homemade version will make a world of difference to the end result.

INGREDIENTS

Thai red curry paste

5 dried red chilies

1 teaspoon coriander seeds

½ teaspoon cumin seeds

1 teaspoon white peppercorns

½ teaspoon shrimp paste

2 coriander (cilantro) roots, cleaned and chopped

1 red Asian shallot (or ½ red onion), peeled and roughly chopped

4 garlic cloves, roughly chopped

1 lemongrass stalk, finely sliced

½ tablespoon minced galangal or ginger

½ tablespoon lime zest (or lemon zest)

1 teaspoon sea salt

1 tablespoon extra virgin olive oil

Butterflied spatchcock

4 x 380 g (13½ oz) free range spatchcock (or poussin)

160 g (5½ oz) red curry paste (above)

125 ml (4 fl oz) coconut milk

1 tablespoon gluten free fish sauce

6 kaffir lime leaves (optional), centre vein removed and finely chopped

Steamed Coconut and Spring Onion Brown Rice (p. 193), to serve

lime wedges, to serve

METHOD

- Preheat oven to 200°C (400°F).
- For the curry paste, soak the chilies in hot water for 30 minutes. Remove from water and finely chop.
- In a medium frying pan, dry roast coriander seeds and cumin seeds over medium-low heat for 2–3 minutes or until fragrant. Transfer cumin and coriander to a mortar and pestle, together with the white peppercorns and grind to a rough powder. Place in a food processor and add the remaining red curry paste ingredients, together with the soaked chilies. Process to a smooth paste. Divide the red curry paste into 2 portions—half to marinate the spatchcock and the remaining half for the curry sauce.
- To butterfly spatchcock, use kitchen scissors to cut down either side of the backbone, then remove (reserve the backbones to make chicken broth). Remove offal and gristle from cavity and discard. On a chopping board, firmly press down on the breastbone to flatten. Using half the red curry paste, pour over the spatchcock and rub to coat. Leave to marinate for at least 30 minutes or overnight in the refrigerator.
- To make the coconut red curry sauce, heat a small saucepan over a medium temperature. Add the remaining curry paste and cook until fragrant. Add coconut milk, fish sauce and kaffir lime leaves. Stirring constantly, cook for 5–6 minutes or until combined.
- Transfer spatchcock to a baking tray large enough to fit spatchcocks in a single layer. Roast for 15 minutes and then turn up the oven to 220°C (425°F) for a further 5 minutes to get the skin crispy. Take the spatchcock out of the oven and rest in a warm place for 5 minutes. Drizzle generously with coconut red curry sauce and serve with Steamed Coconut and Spring Onion Brown Rice and lime wedges.

Note: The homemade red Thai curry paste makes 160 g (5½ oz) or substitute with 100 g (3½ oz) store-bought paste. I love serving individual baby chickens (known as *poussin* or spatchcock) but you can use a whole free range chicken if you wish.

PEKING DUCK BREAST RICE PAPER ROLLS WITH PLUM DIPPING SAUCE

This dish is a shameless fusion of two classic dishes; Vietnamese rice paper rolls and Chinese Peking duck pancakes. Traditionalists may turn up their noses but I think this is a bit of a revelation.

INGREDIENTS

2 x 250 g (9 oz) duck breasts, skin on
½ teaspoon Chinese five spice powder
sea salt and freshly ground black pepper
1 tablespoon extra virgin olive oil

Plum dipping sauce
4– 6 large (about 300 g/10½ oz) fresh or canned plums, halved and stones removed
2 star anise
1 cinnamon quill
1 teaspoon fresh ginger, finely grated
1 long red chili, deseeded and roughly chopped
1 tablespoon runny honey
½ teaspoon sesame oil

Rice paper rolls
100 g (3½ oz) bean thread noodles (cellophane noodles)
12 x 15 cm (6 in) rice paper rounds
1 telegraph cucumber, cut into matchstick-size batons
2 carrots, peeled and cut into matchstick-size batons
3 spring onions (scallions), white part only, thinly sliced lengthways
½ bunch mint leaves
½ bunch coriander (cilantro) leaves

METHOD

- Preheat oven to 180°C (350°F).
- Using a sharp knife, score the skin of the duck in a criss-cross pattern, taking care not to cut into the meat flesh. Using your hands, rub five spice, sea salt and black pepper into the skin.
- To make the dipping sauce, place all the ingredients in a small saucepan and simmer over medium heat. Cook, stirring occasionally, until the sauce thickens slightly and the plums have broken down, about 6–8 minutes. If you'd like a smooth consistency, remove cinnamon quill and star anise and blend sauce in a food processor—I prefer a chunky dipping sauce.
- Heat oil in a large frying pan over a medium-high temperature. Add the duck breasts, skin-side down, and cook for 8–9 minutes or until most of the fat has rendered and the skin is crisp. Flip the duck breast over and cook for a further 1–2 minutes.
- Transfer to a baking tray and roast in the oven for 8 minutes. Reserve any duck fat left in the pan to use the next time you make roast vegetables. Remove duck from the oven and allow to rest, skin side up, for at least 5 minutes. Once rested, cut the duck breasts into 5 mm (¼ in) thick slices.
- Meanwhile, place noodles in a large bowl. Pour enough boiling water over to cover, let stand until softened, about 10 minutes. Drain and set aside.
- To soak the rice paper rolls, fill an edged plate with warm water. Work with 1 rice paper round at a time. Soak rice paper in water, turning occasionally, until just pliable but not limp, about 30 seconds.
- Place on a damp kitchen towel and arrange duck breast slices across the middle of the rice paper round. Add a small handful of bean thread noodles and top with cucumber, carrot, spring onions, mint and coriander. Add a spoonful of plum sauce and fold the bottom of the rice paper over the filling, then fold in ends and roll like a burrito into a tight cylinder. Repeat until all rolls are filled.
- Cover wrapped rolls with a damp kitchen towel until ready to serve. Divide between bowls and serve with remaining plum sauce.

DRUNKEN ROAST CHICKEN
WITH TARRAGON AND BEETROOT TZATZIKI

I constantly yearn for an old-fashioned roast chicken and this Francophile version fits the bill. Roasted in a generous coating of Dijon mustard, white wine and tarragon, the chicken transforms into an herbaceous, aromatic creation. Before you dispose of the chicken bones in the bin, why not keep them and make some Chicken Broth (p. 187)? This recipe is for my friends Karvy and Matty, who love all things French.

INGREDIENTS

1.5 kg (3 lb) large free range chicken, cut into 8 pieces

250 ml (8 fl oz) dry white wine

125 ml (4 fl oz) Chicken Broth (p. 187) or stock/broth of choice

1 tablespoon Dijon mustard

8 garlic cloves, finely chopped

3 tablespoons fresh tarragon, roughly chopped

2 tablespoons fresh thyme, roughly chopped

2 tablespoons parsley, roughly chopped

1 tablespoon extra virgin olive oil

sea salt and freshly ground black pepper

Roasted Mixed Potatoes (p. 157), to serve

Beetroot Tzatziki (p. 186), to serve

METHOD

- Preheat oven to 180°C (350°F).
- Place the chicken pieces in a large deep-sided roasting tray.
- In a bowl, combine the wine, broth, mustard, garlic and herbs and pour over the chicken. Drizzle over olive oil and season with salt and pepper. Roast, uncovered, for 45–50 minutes or until the chicken is just cooked through.
- Serve with roasted mixed potatoes and beetroot tzatziki.

STICKY POMEGRANATE CHICKEN WITH IRANIAN JEWELLED RICE

Jewelled rice is a famous Iranian dish, traditionally served at weddings and it truly does scream of celebration— the butter-and-saffron coated rice is laced with colorful flecks of dried fruit and toasted nuts and glistening strips of citrus zest. It is usually served with barberries but I find them difficult to source, so I substitute with cranberries.

INGREDIENTS

750 g (1 lb 10 oz) free range chicken thigh fillets, sliced lengthways into 3 even sized pieces

2 garlic cloves, finely chopped

1 teaspoon fresh ginger, finely grated

1 teaspoon sesame oil

3 tablespoons pomegranate molasses

1 tablespoon tamari (or light soy sauce)

1 tablespoon extra virgin olive oil

Iranian jewelled rice

150 ml (5 fl oz) coconut milk

250 ml (8 fl oz) water

200 g (7 oz) brown basmati rice, washed and rinsed

pinch of saffron (optional)

2 tablespoons butter or extra virgin olive oil (for dairy free)

2 tablespoons pistachio kernels

2 tablespoons slivered almonds

2 tablespoons cranberries, unsweetened

large pinch of ground cinnamon

large pinch of ground cardamom

large pinch of ground allspice

1 orange zest strip

seeds (arils) from 1 pomegranate

sea salt, to taste

METHOD

- Start by marinating the chicken. Place garlic, ginger, sesame oil, pomegranate molasses, tamari and oil in a bowl. Add chicken and toss to coat. Leave to marinate for at least 30 minutes or overnight if time allows.

- To make the jewelled rice, place the coconut milk, water, basmati and saffron in a medium saucepan. Bring to the boil and stir to combine. Reduce heat to low, cover and simmer for 12–14 minutes. Remove from the heat and set aside, covered, for 5–10 minutes.

- Meanwhile, melt the butter or oil in a medium frying pan. Add the pistachios, almonds, cranberries, spices and orange zest. Cook, stirring constantly, until fragrant, about 1 minute.

- Once the rice has rested, remove the lid and fluff with a fork. Toss buttery nuts, cranberries, spices and zest through the rice. Set aside.

- Heat a large frying pan to a medium temperature. Add chicken, in batches, and cook for about 5 minutes or until caramelized and just cooked through. Remove from the heat and allow to rest, about 3 minutes.

- To serve, spoon the rice into bowls, top with chicken and, at the last minute, scatter with pomegranate arils.

BEEF FILLET AND EGGPLANT CAVIAR
WITH ROASTED MIXED POTATOES AND SALSA VERDE

Cooking a whole beef fillet is definitely for special occasions, especially when it is coupled with the herby pungency of the salsa verde and creamy, chilli-studded eggplant. A key ingredient of the eggplant caviar is the salty (brined) green peppercorns, which can be found at most supermarkets in a jar or tin.

INGREDIENTS

Eggplant caviar

2 large eggplants (aubergines), about 600 g (1 lb 5 oz), halved lengthways

3 tablespoons extra virgin olive oil

3 spring onions (scallions), finely chopped

2 garlic cloves, finely chopped

1 small red chili, finely chopped

1 teaspoon orange zest

3 anchovy fillets, finely chopped

8 canned green peppercorns in brine, crushed

1 tablespoon coriander (cilantro), finely chopped

1 tablespoon flat leaf parsley, finely chopped

1½ tablespoons lemon juice

sea salt and freshly ground black pepper

Beef fillet

2 tablespoons extra virgin olive oil

1 beef fillet (about 1.2 kg/2 lb 10 oz)

sea salt and freshly ground black pepper

Roasted Mixed Potatoes (p. 157), to serve

Salsa Verde (p. 184), to serve

baby herbs of choice, to serve

METHOD

- Preheat oven to 180°C (350°F).
- Score the flesh of the eggplant in a criss-cross pattern and brush with half the oil. Place on a lined baking tray, cut side up and roast for 35–40 minutes. Allow to cool then scoop eggplant flesh out (discarding skin).
- To prepare your beef, remove any tough muscle or connective tissue.
- Tie (or truss) your beef. Place the fillet horizontally in front of you. Cut a 1–1.5 m (3–5 ft) length of butcher's string and starting at one end of the fillet, pass the string underneath the meat, about 3 cm (1¼ in) from the tip, and tie a knot at one end of the length of string. Cross the string over to create a loop and slide this under the meat, pulling the string tight until it is firmly around the fillet, about 3 cm (1¼ in) below the first loop. Continue to truss at 3 cm (1¼ in) intervals. At the final loop, pull the string tight, tie it into a knot and trim the excess string.
- Heat oil in a large frying pan over a high temperature. Generously season beef and cook, turning occasionally, until brown, 1–2 minutes each side. Place on a wire rack over a baking tray and roast at 180°C (350°F), about 35–40 minutes for rare. Cover loosely with foil and set aside to rest.
- To finish the eggplant caviar, add the remaining olive oil in a frying pan over a medium heat. Add spring onions, garlic, chili and orange zest. Cook for 3 minutes or until soft and fragrant. Add anchovies, peppercorns and eggplant. Cook, stirring occasionally, for 2 minutes. Remove from the heat and stir through herbs and lemon juice. Season to taste.
- To serve, thickly slice the beef. Divide Roasted Mixed Potatoes between bowls, arrange beef slices on top. Add eggplant caviar, scatter with salsa verde and baby herbs and drizzle with a little extra olive oil, to serve.

Note: You can roast and drain the eggplant the night before if you wish.

STUFFED TURKEY WITH QUINOA, CRANBERRY AND PISTACHIO STUFFING

In many places around the world, turkey is associated with Christmas fare, but I would happily serve (and eat) this all year around. Stuffing the turkey under the skin (not inside the cavity) leaves the meat gloriously moist which is a great trick—no more dry turkey.

INGREDIENTS

1 x 3–3.5 kg (6–7 lb) turkey

Stuffing
100 g (3½ oz) quinoa, rinsed and
    drained
250 ml (8 fl oz) Chicken Broth (p. 187)
    or stock/broth of choice
2 tablespoons butter or extra virgin
    olive oil (for dairy free)
1 small red onion, peeled and diced
2 garlic cloves, finely chopped
2 celery stalks, chopped
10 sage leaves, roughly chopped
60 g (2 oz) pistachios, chopped
60 g (2 oz) dried cranberries,
    unsweetened
1 teaspoon lemon zest
¼ teaspoon nutmeg
200 g (7 oz) pork mince
1 free range egg
1 large orange
sea salt and freshly ground black pepper

METHOD

- Preheat oven to 220°C (425°F).
- Start by cooking the quinoa. Place quinoa and broth in a small saucepan and bring to the boil. Reduce heat to low, cover and cook until the liquid has been absorbed and the quinoa is tender, about 15 minutes. Uncover, fluff the quinoa with a fork and set aside.
- Heat butter in a frying pan over a medium temperature. Sauté the onion for 2 minutes or until translucent. Add garlic, celery and sage and sauté until softened. Remove from the heat and add pistachios, cranberries, lemon zest and nutmeg. Cool to room temperature before adding pork mince and egg. Stir to combine.
- Dry the turkey with absorbent paper. Place on a chopping board and, starting from the neck, work your fingers under the skin, separating the skin from the breast and thigh meat. Working slowly, you should be able to create a whole pocket (without any holes). Once done, push the stuffing between the skin and meat. Stuff the orange into the cavity of the turkey.
- Place turkey on a large roasting tray. Rub the skin all over with olive oil and season generously. Cover turkey with foil and place in oven. Turn the heat down immediately to 180°C (350°F) and roast for 2 hours 15 minutes. Remove the foil and roast for a further 45 minutes. At this point, you can check if the turkey is cooked by pressing a skewer or knife into the thigh. When the juices run clear, it is cooked.

Note: You can use 230 g (8 oz) cooked quinoa instead of cooking it from scratch.

Side

Kick

These are my modest bowls that work alongside more substantial mains. The Smashed Baby Potatoes with Prosciutto Crackling and Dill Sour Cream Dressing (p. 148) are deserving of a place beside a just-seared rib eye or scotch fillet, while the Barbecue Carrots with Tangy Buttermilk and Dill Dressing (p. 155) will bolster any picnic spread.

In saying that, I have been known to consume the entire serving of Sweet and Sour Asian Brussels Sprouts with Crispy Shallots (p. 147) by myself and, I must warn, the Roasted Cabbage Wedges with Lemon Harissa Dressing (p. 155) will steal the limelight from any dish it's served alongside.

SWEET AND SOUR ASIAN BRUSSELS SPROUTS WITH CRISPY SHALLOTS

To say I'm fond of Brussels sprouts is an understatement. Even as I write this, with dinner already in the oven, I am thinking of ways to justify popping down to the shops to make this dish. Again. These are best enjoyed alongside the Sticky Tamarind, Sesame and Lime Chicken Wings (p. 42).

INGREDIENTS

125 ml (4 fl oz) extra virgin olive oil

3 large golden shallots (French shallots), shaved on a mandolin or thinly sliced

500 g (1 lb 2 oz) small Brussels sprouts, trimmed and cut in half lengthways

1 teaspoon sea salt

½ teaspoon freshly ground black pepper

lime wedges, to serve

Sweet and sour dressing

1 garlic clove

3 small red chilies, coarsely chopped, plus extra to serve

2 tablespoons gluten free fish sauce

METHOD

- Heat oil in a frying pan to a medium-high temperature. Once the pan is hot, add shallots and fry until crisp, about 5 minutes and then transfer with a slotted spoon to absorbent paper to drain.
- Using the oil in the same frying pan, cook Brussels sprouts, in batches, turning occasionally until lightly golden all over. Remove with a slotted spoon and transfer to absorbent paper. Immediately sprinkle with salt and pepper. Repeat until all the Brussels sprouts are golden. You may need to add more oil, depending on the size of your frying pan.
- To make the sweet and sour dressing, place garlic and chilies in a mortar and pestle and pound to a paste. Transfer to a bowl and add fish sauce.
- Place Brussels sprouts in a large serving bowl, drizzle with sweet and sour dressing and toss to combine. Scatter with fried crispy shallots, extra chili (if desired) and serve with lime wedges.

SMASHED BABY POTATOES WITH PROSCIUTTO CRACKLING AND DILL SOUR CREAM DRESSING

This dish is a combination of all of my husband's favorite foods—crispy potatoes, prosciutto and mayonnaise. If only I could somehow include pork ribs into this dish, this would be his last supper. Crunchy on the outside, tender on the inside, this dish features potatoes at their best. You can boil them in advance, just keep them chilled in your refrigerator.

INGREDIENTS

1 kg (2 lb 3 oz) baby potatoes
5 slices gluten free prosciutto, roughly chopped
2 tablespoons extra virgin olive oil

Dill and sour cream dressing

2 tablespoons sour cream
2 tablespoons Whole Egg Mayonnaise (p. 178) or store-bought
1 tablespoon lemon juice
1 tablespoon capers, drained and chopped
1 tablespoon chives, finely sliced, extra to serve

METHOD

- Preheat oven to 200°C (400°F).
- Place potatoes in a large saucepan of salted water and bring to the boil. Reduce the heat to low, cover and cook for 12–14 minutes or until just tender. Test by stabbing the potatoes with a sharp knife or skewer; if the potatoes are still firm, continue cooking. Drain and allow to cool slightly.
- Place potatoes in a large bowl. Add prosciutto and oil and toss to coat.
- Place potatoes on a large lined baking tray and using the back of a fork or the palm of your hand, press or squash the potatoes until they're flattened.
- Roast for 35–40 minutes or until golden and tender, rotating the tray halfway through.
- Combine sour cream, mayonnaise, lemon juice, capers and chives in a small bowl and stir to combine.
- Place crunchy potatoes in a bowl, drizzle with dressing and scatter with extra chives.

Note: There are so many potato varieties available which is why I didn't want to be specific in this recipe—look for ones with a creamy, buttery flesh (check by feeling the potatoes).

CHARRED FENNEL AND CRISPY LEEK WITH KAFFIR LIME AND YOGURT DRESSING

This is intended to be a very light dish—something that doesn't try to share the limelight with a more substantial dish but manages to enhance any and every dish that it's served with.

INGREDIENTS

4 fennel bulbs, quartered and fronds reserved
3 tablespoons extra virgin olive oil
2 leeks, woody end removed, halved lengthways and thinly sliced into half moons
sea salt and freshly ground pepper

Kaffir lime, fennel and yogurt dressing
1 medium zucchini (courgette), grated
1 clove garlic, finely grated
6 fresh kaffir lime leaves, middle vein removed and thinly sliced
reserved fennel fronds, finely chopped
1 tablespoon lemon juice
200 g (7 oz) natural Greek yogurt

METHOD

- Heat a grill pan or barbecue to a medium-high temperature. Brush the fennel with half the olive oil and season with salt and pepper. Once grill is hot, cook fennel, turning occasionally, for about 15–20 minutes or until charred on the outside and tender.
- Meanwhile, heat remaining oil in a large frying pan over a medium-low temperature. Add leek and a pinch of salt and cook, stirring occasionally until the edges get crispy, about 6–8 minutes.
- To make the dressing, place the grated zucchini in a colander with a teaspoon of salt. Leave to drain for about 20 minutes, then squeeze out as much liquid as you can with your hands. Once the zucchini has drained, place in a bowl with remaining ingredients. Stir to combine and season to taste.
- Place charred fennel in a serving bowl, scatter with crispy leek and drizzle with dressing.

Note: If you can't find fresh kaffir lime leaves, you can substitute with dill fronds (double the amount) for this dressing.

COCONUT ROASTED SWEET POTATO WEDGES WITH PICKLED RED ONIONS AND SMOKY CHIPOTLE SAUCE

I could eat this every day, no joke. This should really be called a Netflix bowl because it is the perfect dish to get you through a television series marathon. Vinegary red onion rings with crunchy yet gooey sweet potato wedges—brought together with a smoky and spicy chipotle sauce makes this dish one of my all time favorites. These are great served alongside the Sumac Lamb Chops (p. 133).

INGREDIENTS

Sweet potato wedges

800 g (1 lb 12 oz) orange or purple sweet potato, unpeeled

3 tablespoons coconut oil

1 teaspoon sea salt

½ teaspoon freshly ground black pepper

Pickled red onion

1 red onion, thinly sliced

125 ml (4 fl oz) white wine vinegar

Smoky chipotle sauce

100 g (3½ oz) Whole Egg Mayonnaise (p. 178) or store-bought

1 teaspoon dried chipotle chili flakes

1 tablespoon lime juice

¼ teaspoon smoked paprika

1 teaspoon pure maple syrup (optional)

METHOD

- Preheat oven to 200°C (400°F).
- Cut sweet potato into even sized wedges and place on a lined baking tray in a single layer. Add oil, salt and pepper. Roast until golden and crunchy, about 35–40 minutes, turning halfway through.
- While the sweet potatoes are roasting, make the pickled red onion. Place the onion in a bowl, pour the vinegar over this, making sure the onion is submerged. Set aside to pickle for at least 15 minutes. You can speed up the pickling process by using your hands to massage the vinegar into the onion.
- To make the chipotle sauce, place all the ingredients in a bowl and stir to combine.
- Remove onion slices and discard excess vinegar. (Or, if you're like me and love vinegar, reserve a little of the pickling liquid to scatter on top of the wedges).
- To serve, place sweet wedges in a serving bowl, scatter with pickled red onion and spicy chipotle sauce.

Note: To make this vegetarian and vegan, use vegan mayonnaise.

SALT-AND-VINEGAR POTATO RÖSTI

This does seem more fiddly than many of my recipes however it's a trade-off that I am sure you will be happy to make. This is a crowd-pleaser. To ease the labour, the potatoes can be parboiled a day ahead (once cold, cover) and the rösti itself can constructed ahead of time and then you just need to put it in the oven.

INGREDIENTS

1.5 kg (3 lb) starchy potatoes (Coliban or King Edward), peeled

1 tablespoon sea salt

2 x 24 cm (9½ in) cake tins

2 tablespoons olive oil

2 red onions, thinly sliced

3 tablespoons white vinegar

1 tablespoon sea salt, plus more to season

½ tablespoon rosemary, finely chopped

freshly ground black pepper

METHOD

- Preheat oven to 200°C (400°F).
- Bring a large pot of salted water to the boil. Add potatoes and parboil until a knife slides into the centre of the potato with some resistance, about 15–20 minutes. Drain potatoes, rinse in cold water, cover, and place in the refrigerator until very cold, about 30–40 minutes.
- Grease 2 x 24 cm (9½ in) cake tins with 2 teaspoons of olive oil.
- Place onions, vinegar and 1 tablespoon sea salt in a large bowl. Toss to combine and allow onions to soften, about 10 minutes. To speed up the pickling process, use your hands to toss and massage the onions with vinegar.
- Meanwhile, grate chilled and parboiled potatoes on a box grater or in a food processor.
- Add potatoes and rosemary to pickled onion mixture and toss to combine. Season with pepper.
- Divide potato mixture between cake tins and press down as firmly as possible. Brush the top with the remaining olive oil and place in the oven and bake until the rösti is golden around the edges, about 45–60 minutes. Remove from oven. To crisp up the top of the rösti, brush with more olive oil and place under a griller. Cook until golden, about 5 minutes, then serve.

FRIED BROCCOLI WITH INDIAN SPICED LABNEH

I'm always on the hunt for creative ways to cook readily-available supermarket veggies, such as broccoli. Don't be disparaged by the 'fried' description, the broccoli is merely sautéed in oil until crisp and delectable.

INGREDIENTS

2 heads broccoli (about 500 g/1 lb),
   stems removed and florets halved
2 teaspoons cumin seeds
2 teaspoons fennel seeds
1 teaspoon coriander seeds
100 g (3½ oz) Labneh (p. 183) or 150 g
   (5¼ oz) natural Greek yogurt
½ lemon, juiced
2 tablespoons extra virgin olive oil
3 garlic cloves, roughly chopped
½ teaspoon lemon zest
sea salt and freshly ground black pepper

METHOD

- Bring a medium saucepan of salted water to a boil. Blanch the broccoli until just cooked but still firm to the bite (al dente), about 1–2 minutes. Drain in a colander and set aside.
- Heat a frying pan to a low temperature and add cumin, fennel and coriander seeds. Dry roast until fragrant and aromatic, about 2 minutes. Transfer to a mortar and pestle and crush to a rough powder.
- Place crushed spices, labneh and lemon juice in a bowl. Stir to combine and season to taste.
- Meanwhile, heat oil in a grill pan over a high temperature. Add garlic and lemon zest and stir fry until lightly golden. Add drained broccoli florets and continue to cook until broccoli is lightly charred, about 4 minutes. Season with salt and pepper.
- To serve, place broccoli in a bowl and top with spiced labneh.

Note: For non-vegetarians, this is wonderful served alongside the Indian Spiced Roasted Fish with Red Lentil Dhal (p. 51).

BARBECUE CARROTS
WITH TANGY BUTTERMILK AND DILL DRESSING

I'm the first to admit, carrots don't get me too excited. However, liberally coat them with punchy spices and douse them in a creamy and zingy buttermilk dressing and yes, now we can talk. Parboiling the carrots before you grill them ensures they'll be tender without burning the spice mixture.

INGREDIENTS

1 tablespoon smoked paprika

2 teaspoons ground cumin

2 teaspoons gluten free celery salt

¼ teaspoon cayenne pepper

2 garlic cloves, finely chopped

1 tablespoon sea salt

1 teaspoon freshly ground black pepper

450 g (1 lb) baby carrots, scrubbed, halved lengthways

3 tablespoons extra virgin olive oil

3 tablespoons pistachios, dry roasted, salted, shelled and roughly chopped

Beetroot Tzatziki (p. 186), to serve

Seedy Superfood Crackers (p. 45), to serve

Buttermilk and dill dressing

125 ml (4 fl oz) buttermilk

2 teaspoons Dijon mustard

3 tablespoons fresh dill, chopped

1 tablespoon lemon juice

sea salt and freshly ground black pepper

METHOD

- Combine paprika, cumin, celery salt, cayenne pepper, garlic, salt and black pepper in a bowl.
- Bring a large saucepan of salted water to the boil. Add carrots and cook until tender but still crisp, about 4 minutes. Drain and transfer carrots to a medium bowl.
- Add oil and spice mixture and rub carrots to coat. Cover and leave to marinate, at room temperature, for at least 15 minutes or overnight.
- Meanwhile, whisk all the buttermilk dressing ingredients together in a small bowl and season to taste.
- Heat a barbecue or grill pan to a medium-high temperature. Grill carrots, cut side down, until they are lightly charred and caramelized, about 4–5 minutes.
- Arrange carrots in a bowl, drizzle with dressing and scatter with pistachios. Serve alongside beetroot tzatziki and seedy superfood crackers as part of a nibbles platter.

Note: If you can't buy buttermilk, whisk together 125 ml (4 fl oz) full cream milk with 2 teaspoons of lemon juice. Allow to sit for 5–10 minutes or until the mixture thickens slightly and small curdles form. It won't be as thick as buttermilk, but the taste will be the same.

ROASTED CABBAGE WEDGES
WITH LEMON HARISSA DRESSING

Roasted cabbage is truly a revelation. I'm the self-appointed leader of the roasted cabbage club and have tried my damnedest to convert anyone and everyone. This recipe proves that cabbage is no plain Jane in the vegetable world.

INGREDIENTS

Roasted cabbage
1 Savoy cabbage, cut into wedges
3 tablespoons extra virgin olive oil
3 garlic cloves, finely chopped or grated
    on a fine zester
sea salt and freshly ground pepper

Lemon harissa dressing
3 tablespoons extra virgin olive oil
1 teaspoon lemon zest
2 tablespoons lemon juice
2–3 teaspoons Harissa Paste (p. 190) or
    store-bought harissa paste
2 teaspoons Dijon mustard
2 tablespoons chopped flat leaf parsley

METHOD

- Preheat oven to 200°C (400°F).
- Slice cabbage into even sized wedges about 3 cm (1¼ in) thick at the widest end. Place on a lined baking tray in a single layer and add olive oil, garlic, salt and pepper and toss to coat.
- Roast for 25–30 minutes. Turn the cabbage over and continue cooking for a further 5–10 minutes or until the cabbage is charred and crunchy around the edges.
- Meanwhile, combine all the dressing ingredients in a bowl.
- Place cabbage wedges in a serving bowl and scatter with lemon harissa dressing.

ROASTED MIXED POTATOES

These roasted potatoes are a handy recipe to have up your sleeve because they're simple to make and are the perfect base to absorb bolder, punchier flavors. Served underneath the Drunken Roast Chicken with Tarragon and Beetroot Tzatziki (p. 139), they complete this French-inspired dish but this isn't to say they aren't delicious on their own.

INGREDIENTS

500 g (1 lb 2 oz) baby chat potatoes,
    peeled and halved
500 g (1 lb 2 oz) sweet potatoes, peeled
    and cut into 2 cm (¾ in) cubes
1 red onion, peeled and cut into wedges
3–4 garlic cloves, roughly chopped
    (optional)
handful of herbs such as thyme,
    rosemary or tarragon (optional)
3 tablespoons extra virgin olive oil
sea salt and freshly ground pepper

METHOD

- Preheat oven to 200°C (400°F).
- Spread potatoes, sweet potatoes and red onion wedges in a single layer on a lined baking tray (or two), making sure they're not overcrowded (otherwise they won't crisp up). Add garlic and herbs (if using) and drizzle with olive oil. Season with salt and pepper and toss to coat.
- Roast for 45–50 minutes, tossing every 15 minutes, until golden and tender.

Sweet Bowls

I was once a massive sweet tooth and would devour anything that came my way but as the years creep by, I tend to lean towards salty-sweet or citrus-sweet treats. The Gooey Chocolate and Espresso Puddings (p. 162) in this chapter are tempered by a salted almond brittle while a Strawberry and Balsamic Semifreddo (p. 161) is tossed with balsamic vinegar to cut through the creaminess. Quinces, which are naturally quite tart, are softened and sweetened in a cardamom syrup and served with dollops of luscious Vanilla Mascarpone (p. 167).

I use a minimal amount of sugar in my recipes, preferring natural sweeteners such as honey, maple syrup and Mother Nature's very own source of sugar, fruit, which makes those moments of decadence slightly more wholesome. This isn't to say that these sweeteners aren't sugar (they are), I just choose these sources of sugar as they are less refined. Most of all though, food is meant to be enjoyed so tuck in and enjoy without guilt or restraint.

SIMPLE STRAWBERRY AND BALSAMIC SEMIFREDDO

I can't express my passion for this simple bowl of deliciousness in words. A highlight of my new London home features a bowl of the sweetest strawberries I've ever tasted and nightly bowls of this semifreddo (a partially frozen Italian dessert similar to ice-cream).

INGREDIENTS

50 g (1¾ oz) unsalted butter
100 g (3½ oz) caster (superfine) sugar
400 g (14 oz) fresh or frozen strawberries
2 teaspoons balsamic vinegar
2 free range egg whites
200 ml (7 oz) thickened cream
fresh seasonal berries (blueberries, strawberries, raspberries), to serve
edible flowers, to serve (optional)

METHOD

- Place butter, half the sugar and strawberries in a saucepan over a medium heat. Stirring occasionally, cook until the strawberries have broken down into a thick, chunky jam (they shouldn't be too syrupy), about 10–15 minutes. Stir in vinegar and allow to cool.
- Using hand-held beaters or an electric mixer, whisk egg whites until soft peaks form. With the motor running, add remaining sugar, a tablespoon at a time, whisking until the sugar dissolves, about 4–5 minutes. Gently fold in the cooled strawberry balsamic mixture.
- In a separate bowl, whip the cream until stiff and fold into the strawberry and egg white mixture.
- Spoon into 6 x 250 ml (8 fl oz) bowls or molds (or a 1.5 L/2½ pt foil-lined loaf tin) and place in the refrigerator to set overnight.
- Serve topped with a handful of fresh seasonal berries and edible flowers.

GOOEY CHOCOLATE AND ESPRESSO PUDDINGS WITH SALTED ALMOND BRITTLE

Everyone needs a foolproof, sexy chocolate pudding in their repertoire and this gooey espresso version always delivers. You can easily skip the shot of espresso if you don't have a machine—it won't affect the cooking time or yum factor.

INGREDIENTS

150 g (5¼ oz) butter, chopped, plus extra for greasing
80 g (3 oz) caster (superfine) sugar
150 g (5¼ oz) dark chocolate (70 per cent cocoa solids), roughly chopped
30 ml (1 fl oz) shot of espresso
3 free range egg yolks
3 whole free range eggs
1 tablespoon cornflour (cornstarch), sifted
double cream, to serve

Salted almond brittle
100 g (3½ oz) almond flakes
50 g (1¾ oz) caster (superfine) sugar
50 g (1¾ oz) butter
2 teaspoons sea salt

METHOD

- Preheat oven to 180°C (350°F).
- Grease 4 individual pudding bowls or ovenproof ramekins with butter.
- Place the butter, sugar and chocolate in a heatproof bowl and melt over a saucepan of simmering water. Once melted, remove from the heat. Add espresso and whisk until combined.
- Whisking constantly, add egg yolks and whole eggs, making sure the egg doesn't cook. Fold in cornflour.
- Pour mixture into prepared bowls and place onto a baking tray. Put straight into the oven and cook for 16–18 minutes.
- Meanwhile, to make the salted almond brittle, heat a large non-stick frying pan to a medium-low temperature. Add almonds, caster (superfine) sugar, butter and salt. Heat, stirring constantly, until lightly golden and the sugar has dissolved and caramelized the almonds. Remove from pan and spread in a single layer on a plate lined with baking (parchment) paper. Allow to cool and then gently break up with your hands.
- Allow puddings to rest for a minute or so before serving with double cream and topped with salted almond brittle.

FRESH MINT, MILK CHOCOLATE AND YOGURT MOUSSE

If you promised your guests chocolate mousse, this is certainly not what they would have in mind. Think of this more as a choc-mint whipped cream that sets into a less dense mousse-like consistency. You will need to eat this as soon as you fold through the mint leaves (otherwise they will go brown). But if you insist on making this ahead of time, blanch the mint in boiling water for just a second and refresh in ice water before folding through the mousse (this way, the mint will remain bright green and retain its flavor.)

INGREDIENTS

250 ml (8 fl oz) pure single cream
250 g (9 oz) natural Greek yogurt
100 g (3½ oz) good quality milk
  chocolate, roughly chopped
½ bunch mint, finely chopped

METHOD

- Place cream in a clean mixing bowl and, using hand held beaters or an electric mixer, whisk until stiff peaks form.
- In a large bowl, add yogurt and milk chocolate and stir to combine. Fold through whipped cream, making sure the milk chocolate is distributed evenly. Just before serving, fold through mint. Divide between bowls and eat immediately.

NANNY'S SELF SAUCING LEMON DELICIOUS PUDDING

I'm sure everyone's grandmother has baked one of these puddings at some stage but my Nanny's recipe is particularly good. It isn't called lemon delicious for no reason—around the edges is a feather-like sponge with a gooey, citrus sauce in the middle that tenderly coats each mouthful. My grandmother says that it's traditionally served warm (but not straight from the oven) and the cream is mandatory. She's right on both counts, of course.

INGREDIENTS

2 free range eggs, separated

2 tablespoons butter, softened

125 g (4½ oz) sugar

1 teaspoon lemon zest

80 ml (2¾ fl oz) lemon juice

2 tablespoons cornflour (cornstarch)

¼ teaspoon gluten free baking powder

250 ml (8 fl oz) milk

pure (single) cream, to serve

icing (confectioners') sugar, to serve

METHOD

- Preheat oven to 180°C (350°F).
- Grease a square 17 cm (7 in) ovenproof dish with butter.
- Using hand-held beaters or an electric mixer, whisk egg whites until soft peaks form.
- In a separate bowl, again using beaters or an electric mixer, cream butter and sugar. Add egg yolks, lemon zest, juice, cornflour, baking powder and milk. Beat to combine and then, using a spatula or wooden spoon, fold through stiff egg whites.
- Pour pudding into the prepared ovenproof dish and place this in a deep roasting pan. Fill the outer roasting pan with water until it is 1 cm (½ in) deep.
- Place in oven and bake until it is golden and just set, about 40 minutes. Remove from the oven and allow to cool in the water bath for about 20 minutes. The pudding will continue to cook.
- Dust generously with icing sugar and serve warm with cream.

QUINCES POACHED IN CARDAMOM SYRUP WITH VANILLA MASCARPONE

Quinces have a mythical beauty—fresh from the tree they're almost inedible yet when they're cooked, they transform into one of the most glorious and luxurious of desserts. Cooks spend much of their time selling recipes based on their speed and ease—this recipe is not one of them; quinces require quite a bit of tender love and care before they can yield their glory. Here, the sugar, cardamom and cinnamon coax any hint of astringency from the quinces, leaving a sweetly scented broth to scoop up the jelly-like texture of the fruit.

INGREDIENTS

1.5 L (2½ pt) water
250 g (9 oz) sugar
thinly peeled rind of ½ lemon, white
    pith removed
1 cinnamon quill
6 green cardamom pods, gently crushed
4 quinces (about 1 kg/2 lb total,
    unpeeled)

Vanilla mascarpone
125 g (4½ oz) mascarpone
1 vanilla pod, split and seeds scraped
1 teaspoon orange zest, finely grated

METHOD

- Start by preparing the poaching liquid. Place water, sugar, lemon rind, cinnamon and cardamom in a large heavy-based saucepan.
- To prepare the quinces, start by washing them, to rub off all the fur. Peel quinces, then quarter and core and then add immediately to the poaching liquid to prevent discoloration. Bring liquid to a boil, stirring until the sugar dissolves. Reduce heat to a simmer, cover and cook for about 3 hours or until the quinces are tender and ruby red. The cooking time will vary, depending on the quince. They're done when they are cooked through, which you can check by piercing the flesh with the tip of a sharp paring knife. It's not unusual for them to take up to 3½ hours or more.
- Meanwhile, combine mascarpone and scraped vanilla seeds in a bowl. Sprinkle with orange zest, to taste.
- Serve quinces with a little of the warm syrup along with vanilla mascarpone.

Note: Quinces ripen from the inside out so it is better to cook them at the start of the season and store in an airtight container in the freezer until you want to use them.

PAVLOVA PARFAITS WITH COCONUT LIME CREAM, BANANA, KIWIFRUIT AND PASSIONFRUIT

I often find pavlova tooth-achingly sweet so I've ditched the cream and replaced it with a layer of lime-infused whipped coconut. With the leftover egg yolks, you can whip up some Whole Egg Mayonnaise (p. 178), the Gooey Chocolate and Espresso Puddings with Salted Almond Brittle (p. 162) or the Peach, White Chocolate and Macadamia Tartlets (p. 170).

INGREDIENTS

6 free range egg whites, at room
  temperature
pinch of sea salt
300 g (10½ oz) caster (superfine) sugar
1 tablespoon cornflour (cornstarch),
  plus extra for dusting
1 teaspoon apple cider vinegar
1 teaspoon vanilla extract

Coconut lime cream
2 x 400 ml (14 fl oz) tins coconut milk,
  chilled overnight
zest of ½ lime
1 banana, peeled and thinly sliced (or
  any seasonal fruit)
3 kiwifruit, peeled and diced
3 passionfruit, pulp scooped out

METHOD

- Preheat oven to 100°C (225°F).
- Line a large tray with baking (parchment) paper and dust with a little extra cornflour.
- Using hand-held beaters or an electric mixer, whisk egg whites and salt until stiff peaks form. With motor running, add sugar, a tablespoon at a time, whisking until sugar dissolves, around 4–5 minutes. Fold in cornflour, vinegar and vanilla.
- Transfer to prepared tray, shaping the meringue into a 20 cm (8 in) diameter circle, gently smoothing around the edges and making sure the top is flat.
- Bake in the middle of the oven for 3 hours. At this point, turn off the oven and leave to cool completely with the door closed.
- For the coconut lime cream, scoop off the solid top layer of 'cream' from the tins of coconut milk and place cream in a clean bowl. Reserve the remaining coconut milk in the tin to make something like Lemongrass and Turmeric Seafood Curry (p. 67). Using hand-held beaters or an electric mixer, whisk for 1–2 minutes or until it thickens to the same consistency as whipped cream. Stir through the lime zest.
- At this point, you may prefer to serve the pavlova whole—simply spread the coconut lime cream on top and scatter with fruit. If making parfaits, gently break up the pavlova into meringue pieces with your hands. Assemble 6–8 glass jars or bowls and layer the meringue shards, lime cream and fruit, building up to the top of the jar/bowl, reserving a little fruit for the top. Serve immediately.

Note: When choosing your coconut milk, select a brand that has no additives (otherwise it won't set in the refrigerator).

PEACH, WHITE CHOCOLATE AND MACADAMIA TARTLETS

These utterly delicious tartlets were created for my friends, Cec and Toolie. Each component is flexible—swap the white chocolate for dark chocolate, the peaches for apricots or the ricotta for cream.

INGREDIENTS	METHOD
Tart shells	• Preheat oven to 150°C (300°F).
70 g (2½ oz) unsalted macadamias	• Place macadamias on a baking tray and dry roast for 5 minutes or until lightly golden. Remove and set aside to cool slightly.
20 g (¾ oz) shredded coconut	
60 g (2 oz) almond meal (ground almonds)	• Place cooled macadamias, coconut, almond meal, maple syrup, coconut oil and egg yolk in a food processor and blend until it forms a pastry dough.
1 tablespoon pure maple syrup	
2 tablespoons coconut oil, melted	• Spoon the dough into a lightly greased 8-mold muffin tin (molds 125 ml (4 fl oz), pressing the mixture into the base and about 3 cm (1¼ in) up the sides of each mold. Prick the bases with a fork and cook for 10–12 minutes or until lightly golden. Allow to cool in the tin before carefully transferring to a wire rack.
1 free range egg yolk	
vanilla ice-cream, to serve	
Filling	• Melt chocolate in a double boiler, over a gentle heat. Stir gently and once softened, remove from heat.
120 g (4 oz) white chocolate	
100 g (3½ oz) Fresh Ricotta (p. 182) or store-bought	• Fold through ricotta, not mixing completely. Fill tarts with ricotta and white chocolate and then arrange with peach slices.
1–2 ripe yellow peaches (300 g/10½ oz), de-stoned and thinly sliced	• Place tarts in individual serving bowls and serve with your favorite vanilla ice-cream.

Note: This dessert is delicious served with vanilla bean ice-cream, a recipe which is in my first cookbook, *Bowl & Fork*.

CASHEW, DATE AND CARAMEL SLICE CUPS

Everyone has a soft spot for caramel slice. The base of this slice is delicious as it is—I often find myself keeping a small handful just to nibble on (which I wouldn't suggest as the base does become rather thin). Tahini makes up the bulk of the caramel and there is just a scant amount of maple syrup as the dates make the slice sweet enough.

INGREDIENTS

Base
7–8 Medjool dates, seeds removed and
    roughly chopped
80 g (3 oz) dry roasted cashews
80 g (3 oz) dry roasted almonds
2 tablespoons water
1 teaspoon vanilla extract

Caramel
140 g (5 oz) tahini (or any nut butter)
3 tablespoons coconut oil, melted
3 tablespoons pure maple syrup
pinch of sea salt

Chocolate topping
200 g (7 oz) good quality dark chocolate
1 teaspoon coconut oil

Coconut Lime Cream (p. 168) or
    vanilla ice-cream/double cream, to
    serve

METHOD

- Place dates, cashews, almonds, water and vanilla in a food processor. Blend until combined, about 3–4 minutes. Spoon mixture into a 12-cup, non-stick mini muffin tin. Press evenly into the base of each cup.
- Next, prepare the caramel layer. Add tahini, coconut oil, maple syrup and salt to the food processor (there's no need to clean it after preparing the base) and blend until combined. Pour caramel over the bases and place in the refrigerator to set for 20–30 minutes.
- Meanwhile, melt chocolate and oil in the top of a double boiler or in a glass bowl set above a small saucepan of simmering water. Pour melted chocolate over each caramel filling and spread evenly.
- Return to the refrigerator for at least 1 hour or until set. If it still seems a bit soft, return to the refrigerator (or freezer) for a bit longer.
- Serve in a bowl with Coconut Lime Cream (or vanilla ice-cream or double cream).

Note: Make sure the chocolate is dairy free, vegan or vegetarian. You can also serve this as a slice. Use a square 20 cm (8 in) baking tin lined with baking (parchment) paper.

 These cups make a great afternoon tea treat or as a dessert canapé (perfect to pick up in your hands). If using ice-cream or double cream, this dish will no longer be dairy free, vegan or paleo.

FLOURLESS CARROT AND PINEAPPLE CAKE WITH LEMON THYME SYRUP AND LABNEH

My beautiful granny Jane used to make a sweet potato cake very similar to this recipe and every time I make this recipe, I think of her. The crushed pineapple keeps the cake moist and it freezes surprisingly well if you don't eat the entire cake in one sitting (as tends to happen in our house). There's a scant amount of honey in the syrup so it isn't thick—it is more of an aromatic, fresh soup for the cake to swim in.

INGREDIENTS

210 g (7½ oz) almond meal (ground almonds)
80 g (3 oz) shredded coconut
1 teaspoon sea salt
1 teaspoon gluten free bicarbonate of soda (baking powder)
2 teaspoons ground cinnamon
1 teaspoon ground ginger
1 teaspoon mixed spice
110 g (3¾ oz) sultanas
100 g (3½ oz) walnuts, roughly chopped
125 ml (4 fl oz) honey
60 ml (2 fl oz) coconut oil
5 large free range eggs
225 g (8 oz) tin crushed pineapple, with syrup
200 g (7 oz) carrots, peeled and grated
Labneh (p. 183), to serve
lemon zest, to serve

Lemon thyme syrup
250 ml (8 fl oz) water
2 teaspoons lemon zest
3 tablespoons lemon juice
3–4 tablespoons honey
large handful fresh lemon thyme (or thyme), plus extra to serve

METHOD

- Preheat oven to 180°C (350°F).
- Line the base of a lightly greased 22.5 cm (9 in) spring form cake tin with baking (parchment) paper and set aside.
- In a large bowl, combine all dry ingredients: almond meal, shredded coconut, salt, baking powder, cinnamon, ginger, mixed spice, sultanas and walnuts. Stir to combine.
- In a small saucepan, heat honey and coconut oil over a low temperature until runny.
- In a separate bowl, combine eggs, pineapple (including the syrup) and carrots. Add this to the dry ingredients and stir to combine. Pour warm runny honey and coconut oil over and stir quickly to ensure the eggs don't cook.
- Spoon mixture into the prepared cake tin and bake for 1 hour or until just cooked.
- To make the syrup, place the water, lemon zest, juice, honey and lemon thyme in a small saucepan over a medium heat. Stir until the honey dissolves and the sauce thickens slightly, about 5 minutes. Taste and adjust sweetness as required.
- Once the cake has cooled, place a wedge in each serving bowl and surround in a pool of syrup. Add a generous dollop of labneh, top with extra thyme and lemon zest and sprinkle with chopped walnuts.

Note: You can substitute the honey in the lemon thyme syrup with pure maple syrup, agave nectar, brown rice syrup or stevia sweetener if you prefer.

NO-BAKE YOGURT AND MANGO CHEESECAKE POTS WITH CASHEW COCONUT CRUST

I can take or leave anything to do with chocolate (sorry don't hate me!) but a tangy layer of yogurt and cream cheese combined with a buttery, crumbly crust, this is the type of dessert I crave. Top with whatever fruit is in season.

INGREDIENTS

Base

200 g (7 oz) dry roasted cashews, unsalted

90 g (3¼ oz) desiccated (or shredded) coconut

160 g (5½ oz) fresh dates (or dried dates/ figs soaked in water to soften), pitted

½ teaspoon cinnamon

½ teaspoon sea salt

Cheesecake

1 tablespoon powdered gelatine

125 ml (4 fl oz) hot water

520 g (1 lb 2 oz) natural Greek yogurt

250 g (9 oz) cream cheese, softened

250 ml (8 fl oz) coconut cream

1 teaspoon vanilla extract

1 lemon, juiced (or to taste)

180 g (6¼ oz) honey

To decorate

1 punnet fresh raspberries

1 punnet fresh blueberries

1 mango, thinly sliced into ribbons

2 passionfruit, pulp scooped out

edible flowers (optional)

METHOD

- In a food processor, combine all the base ingredients and blitz until the mixture begins to stick together. Press firmly into the bottom of 6 x 250 ml (8 fl oz) pots (about 1 cup), jars or bowls to create an even base and place in the refrigerator.
- In a small bowl, combine powdered gelatine with the hot water. Stir to dissolve.
- In a food processor, combine yogurt, cream cheese, coconut cream, vanilla, lemon juice, honey and dissolved gelatine mixture and process until smooth and creamy. Divide between each of your pots and leave to set in refrigerator for at least 4 hours or overnight.
- To serve, decorate with fresh, plump raspberries, blueberries, curls of mango and passionfruit pulp (or seasonal fruit of your choice).

Note: If you want to make a cake instead, line the base of a lightly greased 22.5 cm (9 in) spring form tin with non-stick baking (parchment) paper. Evenly press the base into the tin and then top with cheesecake before setting in the refrigerator.

Bowl Basics

Emphasising a diet rich in whole foods really is a return to a traditional cook's kitchen. Making your own basics means that you know exactly what is going into the recipe thus avoiding preservatives and excess salt and refined sugar.

While I would love to say that everything you cook can be made quickly, it is not always the case. A good broth, for example, will certainly take some time and making Whole Egg Mayonnaise (p. 178) from scratch is undoubtedly less convenient than picking up a bottle of the store-bought variety.

For me, cooking is pure bliss. There is nothing in life that I enjoy more. However I appreciate that this is not the case for everyone. It's why I try to keep my dishes as simple as possible—the most common feedback I receive is that all my recipes are easy to follow. In saying that, if you don't enjoy cooking, view it more as an investment in your health. As Hippocrates once said, "Let food be thy medicine and medicine be thy food."

WHOLE EGG MAYONNAISE

Don't be scared of mayo! It really does get a bad rap but when you make it yourself, it's simply eggs and oil. Before you start, make sure all your ingredients are at room temperature, as this helps emulsification. Homemade mayonnaise doesn't last as long as store-bought mayonnaise but I think that just shows that it's good for you—it's made with fresh, whole ingredients without any additives to extend its shelf life.

INGREDIENTS

3 garlic cloves, finely chopped
½ teaspoon sea salt
3 small anchovy fillets
1 free range egg yolk
1 whole free range egg
1 teaspoon Dijon mustard
125 ml (4 fl oz) extra virgin olive oil
125 ml (4 fl oz) rice bran oil
1–2 tablespoons lemon juice

METHOD

- Place garlic, salt and anchovies in a food processor and blitz to a paste. Add egg yolk, whole egg and Dijon mustard. Process again.
- With the motor running, gradually add the oil (olive and rice bran), drop by drop at first, then in a thin, steady stream until thick and emulsified.
- Once the oil is combined, add the lemon juice. Season to taste.
- Transfer any mayonnaise not being used immediately to a clean, sealed jar.

Note: Homemade mayonnaise will keep for about 1 week in the refrigerator. To make this vegetarian, leave out the anchovies.

CHIMICHURRI

This is an Argentinian sauce traditionally served with barbecued meat or fish. I find myself serving it with everything and anything. I'm a cook guided by instinct, not strategy, so I encourage you to play around with different herbs.

INGREDIENTS

2 garlic cloves, finely chopped
½ bunch flat leaf parsley, finely chopped
½ bunch coriander (cilantro), finely chopped
3 tablespoons extra virgin olive oil
1 tablespoon red wine vinegar
½ teaspoon dried chili flakes
handful of fresh oregano leaves, finely chopped
sea salt and freshly ground black pepper

METHOD

- Place all the ingredients in a small bowl. Stir to combine and season to taste with salt and pepper.
- Store in the refrigerator, no longer than 24 hours, until ready to eat.

FRESH CASHEW MILK

Fresh cashew milk is surprisingly simple to make but it does require a little forward planning to soak the cashews. I've always looked at nut milk recipes and thought it was criminal to throw away all that nut pulp—it seemed not only expensive but an absolute waste of all those nutritious, delicious flecks of nut. I prefer the taste and substantial texture of this unstrained cashew milk, plus you don't waste a thing. You can leave out the maple syrup—it is still creamy and delicious without it.

INGREDIENTS	METHOD
140 g (5 oz) raw cashews 1 L (2 pt) water plus more for soaking 2 teaspoons pure maple syrup (honey or agave nectar), optional 2 teaspoons vanilla extract ¼ teaspoon ground cinnamon powder pinch of sea salt	• Place cashews in a bowl and cover with extra water. Soak for at least 4 hours or overnight in the refrigerator. • Drain cashews and rinse with cold water until the water runs clear. • Place soaked cashews and 1 L (2 pt) water in a food processor or place in a bowl and use a high-powered stick blender. Blend on high speed until completely smooth and frothy. • Add maple syrup, vanilla, cinnamon and salt and blend to combine. If your blender can't totally break down the cashews, strain the milk through a fine mesh strainer or cheesecloth. • Pour into a glass jar or bottle and store in the refrigerator. It should keep for 3 to 4 days.

ROASTED ALMOND BUTTER

Making your own almond butter is easy—you just need raw almonds, a food processor and a little patience. If you have roasted almonds on hand, skip the roasting step in the method.

INGREDIENTS	METHOD
250 g (9 oz) whole raw almonds	• Preheat oven to 180°C (350°F).
	• Spread almonds on a baking tray and place in the oven for 10 minutes. Remove, stir and continue roasting for a further 5–10 minutes or until lightly golden. Remove and allow to cool on the tray.
	• Place almonds in a food processor and blend to combine, about 30 seconds. Using a spatula, scrape down the sides and continue to blend for about 10 minutes or until the oils from the almonds release and they start to stick together to create a gloriously smooth and creamy consistency.
	• Store in an airtight jar in the refrigerator for up to a month.

Note: You can use cashews, peanuts or other nuts to make your own nut butter.

FRESH RICOTTA

Ricotta is such a versatile ingredient and making it from scratch is not only creamier than many store-bought varieties but it's also a cinch to do. Once I make a batch, I toss it through salads, a warm bowl of pasta or simply serve it drizzled with honey and scattered with crumbled walnuts. It is great as part of a cheese platter too—simply add grated garlic and a generous glug of extra virgin olive oil.

INGREDIENTS

75 ml (2½ fl oz) white vinegar
180 ml (6 fl oz) water
1 L (2 pt) full cream milk
1 teaspoon sea salt

METHOD

- In a small pouring jug, combine the vinegar and water. Set aside.
- Place the milk and salt in a saucepan over medium heat. Stirring constantly, bring to the point of boiling, but do not boil. Remove saucepan from heat. In a slow, steady, circular stream (beginning in the middle and then working out towards the edges), pour the combined vinegar and water into the milk.
- Let the milk sit, undisturbed, for a few minutes or until the milk has separated to form clumps of milky white curds (ricotta).
- Set a strainer over a bowl and line the strainer with cheesecloth or muslin.
- Use a slotted spoon to lift the ricotta clumps and transfer to the strainer.
- Leave the ricotta to drain for 10–60 minutes. Ricotta will keep in the refrigerator for 2–4 days.

Note: You can keep the whey left in the saucepan (after straining the ricotta) to use in the bath. It's great for your skin. You can also make pickles and fermented vegetables with the whey.

LABNEH

Labneh is a creamy, thick Middle Eastern yogurt cheese that is amazingly versatile. It is made by simply straining the whey out of yogurt and the longer you strain it, the thicker it gets. I use it tossed through salads, as a toast spread, as a dip with warm pita bread or as part of a dessert platter.

INGREDIENTS

1 kg (2 lb 3 oz) natural Greek yogurt
½ teaspoon sea salt
extra virgin olive oil

METHOD

- Line a strainer with 2 layers of cheesecloth or muslin cloth and set over a large bowl.
- In another bowl, combine the yogurt and salt, stirring to combine. Pour the yogurt into the lined strainer.
- Fold the ends of the cheesecloth or muslin cloth over the yogurt and allow to drain, in the refrigerator, for a minimum of 4 hours, which will leave you with a creamy, spread consistency, or up to 72 hours, in which time the labneh will be very thick, dense and quite tart.
- Remove the strained cheese (labneh) from the cloth, reserving the liquid (whey) left in the bottom of the bowl.
- To serve, place in a bowl and drizzle with olive oil.

Note: You can use the whey to make sauerkraut, fermented veggies or pickles.

SALSA VERDE

This Italian sauce is on regular rotation in our house and has been so for quite a few years—I'm yet to find a condiment that beats it.

INGREDIENTS

½ bunch flat leaf parsley leaves, roughly chopped
½ bunch basil leaves, roughly chopped
2 anchovy fillets, roughly chopped
1 teaspoon baby capers
1 garlic clove, finely chopped
2 tablespoons extra virgin olive oil
1 tablespoon lemon juice, to taste
1 tablespoon red wine vinegar
sea salt and freshly ground pepper

METHOD

- Place all the ingredients in a food processor and blend until it reaches a smooth consistency. If you don't have a food processor, finely chop all ingredients and stir to combine. Taste and adjust lemon juice and seasoning accordingly.
- Store in the refrigerator, no longer than 24 hours, until ready to eat.

Note: To make it vegetarian or vegan, simply leave out the anchovy fillets and add a little more salt.

QUICK GARLICKY HUMMUS

It may be unusual to microwave your undrained chickpeas before processing but this little trick is genius. I'm not sure of the exact science behind this technique however the garlic seems to infuse the chickpeas and they become rich and creamy. Admittedly, I don't normally encourage using canned ingredients but I can't apologise for speed or ease when the outcome is just the same (if not better). Feel free to use dried chickpeas, soaked overnight and cooked. You can also use roasted garlic or confit garlic instead of raw.

INGREDIENTS

1 x 400 g (14 oz) tin chickpeas, drained
4–5 garlic cloves, roughly chopped
3 tablespoons hulled tahini
3 tablespoons lemon juice
1 teaspoon ground cumin
1 teaspoon sea salt
2 tablespoons extra virgin olive oil

METHOD

- Place undrained chickpeas (including the liquid in the tin) and garlic in a large bowl. Cover the bowl with a plate or silicon cover and microwave on low, for 5 minutes. Covering the bowl will contain any chickpeas that burst and avoid making a mess of your microwave.
- Transfer to a food processor and add the tahini, lemon juice, cumin and salt. Blend until combined. With the motor running, add the olive oil in a steady stream. Process until creamy and smooth. Set aside to allow to cool to room temperature, then place in the refrigerator to thicken.

Note: This hummus gets better with time so if you can make it the day before, the flavors will have time to develop. It can be refrigerated for up to 5 days.

BEETROOT TZATZIKI

The key to a great tzatziki is stripping the cucumber of all its moisture so it remains crunchy and fresh. I love the earthy sweetness that beetroot brings to this classic Greek condiment.

INGREDIENTS

200 g (7 oz) fresh baby beetroot, trimmed

1 Lebanese cucumber, grated

1 teaspoon sea salt

200 g (7 oz) natural Greek yogurt

1 garlic clove, finely chopped

1 tablespoon lemon juice

METHOD

- Preheat oven to 180°C (350°F).
- Wrap each beetroot bulb in foil. Spread on a baking tray and cook for 45–50 minutes or until tender. Check if it's cooked by piercing the beetroot with a skewer—no resistance means it's ready. Once cooked, allow to cool then use plastic gloves to peel and grate the beetroot. Set aside.
- Meanwhile, place the cucumber and salt in a colander and allow to drain for 10 minutes. Squeeze to remove any excess liquid and place in a bowl. Add remaining ingredients, including the grated beetroot, stir to combine and season to taste.
- Store in the refrigerator, no longer than 24 hours, until ready to eat.

Note: If your beetroot has its leaves attached, don't throw them away. They make beautiful leaves to toss through a salad or cook like you would spinach——with a little butter and olive oil in a pan.

CHICKEN BROTH

Broths and stocks have always been a central part of kitchens around the world thanks to their ability to comfort, nourish and heal. Please take this recipe as more of a suggestion—you can honestly throw in whatever you have in the refrigerator or garden. My mother is obsessed with making homemade chicken broth (or stock), however beef or lamb are both delicious too. You can freeze any leftover broth, which particularly comes in handy when making soups and risottos—both of which really benefit from using quality, homemade broth.

INGREDIENTS

1 kg (2 lb 3 oz) free range chicken necks/chicken carcasses (roughly chopped)

2 brown onions, skin on, roughly chopped

2 carrots, skin on, roughly chopped

1 leek, white part only, roughly chopped

2 celery sticks, including leaves, roughly chopped

2 fresh bay leaves

8 white peppercorns

1 sprig fresh thyme

2 sprigs flat leaf parsley, roughly chopped

METHOD

- In a large stockpot, combine all the ingredients and cover with cold water until the water reaches 5 cm (2 in) above the ingredients. Bring slowly to a simmer. When the broth just starts to bubble, skim off any froth from the top using a ladle. Reduce the heat to a gentle simmer, cover and cook for at least 3 hours (or up to 12). The longer you allow your broth to simmer, the better.
- Pass through a large sieve and discard the chicken, vegetables and herbs. Allow broth to cool and remove any fat that has risen to the surface. Store broth in an airtight container. It will keep refrigerated for up to 3 days and frozen for up to 1 month.

Note: You can also add a tablespoon of apple cider vinegar, as this helps to extract minerals from the meat bones. To make different broths, use any beef or lamb bones, bone marrow or any bones leftover from a roast. If using beef bones, simmer for at least 8 hours or up to 24 hours.

VEGETABLE BROTH

Like I've mentioned for the chicken broth, please just use whatever vegetables and herbs that you have on hand. Simply brush off any visible dirt on the vegetables and give them a rough chop. You don't even need to peel them and yes, the onion skin is not a typo—chuck it all in! I keep a big, sealable bag in the freezer and whenever I have any drab veggies or the odds and ends of herbs or leeks, I throw them in the bag to make broth.

INGREDIENTS

2 L (4 pt) cold water
4 garlic cloves, peeled
2 brown onions, skin on, roughly chopped
2 carrots, skin on, roughly chopped
1 leek, white part only, roughly chopped
2 celery sticks with leaves, roughly chopped
2 fresh bay leaves
8 white peppercorns or black peppercorns
1 sprig fresh thyme
1 dried shiitake mushroom
2 sprigs flat leaf parsley, roughly chopped

METHOD

- In a large stockpot, combine all the ingredients and bring slowly to a simmer. When the broth just starts to bubble, reduce the heat to a gentle simmer, cover and cook for 1 hour. Stir occasionally to circulate the vegetables.
- Pass through a large sieve and discard the vegetables and herbs. Allow broth to cool to room temperature then refrigerate stock until chilled.
- Store in airtight container for up to a week in the refrigerator or up to 12 months in the freezer.

TANDOORI SPICE MIX

Tandoori holds a high place in Indian gastronomic lore with recipes being handed down from generation to generation, so I can only hope that this recipe does it justice. I do understand that making spice mixes like this can be tedious and, in the short term, the effort-to-reward ratio seems low however, let me assure you, a great tandoori spice mix is a gift that keeps on giving.

INGREDIENTS

2 teaspoons ground cumin

2 teaspoons ground coriander

2 teaspoons ground turmeric

2 teaspoons paprika

2 teaspoons sea salt

1 teaspoon cayenne pepper

1 teaspoon ground ginger

METHOD

- Add all the spice mix ingredients to a small bowl and stir to combine. Store in an airtight container at room temperature.

Note: This spice mix will last for up to 2 weeks in an airtight container.

HARISSA PASTE

We all know that homemade pastes are best but I promise you, you won't regret putting in the extra effort with this harissa paste. Widely used in Moroccan and Israeli cooking, harissa is a spiced chili paste that actually originated in Tunisia. You can buy harissa paste from most supermarkets, gourmet grocers and delicatessens but each brand varies in quality and taste.

INGREDIENTS

4 long red dried chilies
1 tablespoon cumin seeds
1 tablespoon coriander seeds
2 teaspoons paprika
½ teaspoon cayenne pepper
¼ teaspoon sea salt
2 garlic cloves, finely grated
3 tablespoons extra virgin olive oil
1 tablespoon fresh lemon juice

METHOD

- Place chilies in a bowl and cover with boiling water. Set aside to soften for about 20 minutes.
- Gently heat a small frying pan. Add cumin seeds and coriander seeds and dry roast, stirring constantly, until fragrant, about 2 minutes.
- Remove from heat and place the seeds in a mortar and pestle. Crush until the mixture resembles a ground spice.
- Once dried chilies have softened, remove from water. At this point you can either remove the chili seeds if you would prefer a more mild paste. I enjoy spice so I tend to leave the seeds in. Place chilies in the mortar and pestle and pound until the chili has broken down.
- Place grounds seeds and chili in a bowl with paprika, cayenne, salt, garlic, olive oil and lemon juice. Stir until smooth. Alternatively, place in a food processor and blend until combined.
- Store in an airtight jar and it will keep in the refrigerator for up to 2 months.

CURRY POWDER

Many store-bought curry powders are absurdly high in salt and often the spices themselves aren't very fresh—having being crushed and left to sit in a spice jar for far too long. Making your own not only gives you the flexibility to create a mixture that suits your taste, but it's infinitely tastier.

INGREDIENTS

1 tablespoon coriander seeds

1 tablespoon fennel seeds

1 tablespoon cumin seeds

½ teaspoon white peppercorns

½ teaspoon ground ginger

½ teaspoon ground turmeric

½ teaspoon ground cinnamon

¼ teaspoon sea salt

¼ teaspoon cayenne pepper (optional)

METHOD

- Gently heat a small frying pan. Add coriander seeds, fennel seeds, cumin seeds and white peppercorns and dry roast, stirring constantly until fragrant, about 2 minutes.
- Remove from heat and place toasted seeds in a mortar and pestle. Crush until the mixture resembles a ground spice. Add remaining spices and stir until smooth.
- Store in an airtight jar for up to 2 months.

TWICE-COOKED CRUNCHY GARLIC QUINOA

I know, I know—I'm like you, as soon as I see 'twice cooked' anything, I balk. It seems over complicated but, I promise, it's not and this is coming from someone who makes a point of simplifying everything. The flavor from the coconut oil is beautifully subtle. If I'm feeling a bit run down, I add some ginger and a bit more garlic. And I think spring onions make everything taste better.

INGREDIENTS

190 g (6½ oz) white quinoa, rinsed and drained
500 ml (16 fl oz) Chicken Broth (p. 187) or any stock/broth or water
2 tablespoons coconut or extra virgin olive oil
4–5 garlic cloves, finely chopped
3 spring onions (scallions), finely sliced
sea salt and freshly ground black pepper, to taste

METHOD

- Place quinoa and broth in a saucepan and bring to the boil. Reduce heat, cover and cook until the liquid has been absorbed and the quinoa is tender, about 15 minutes. Uncover, fluff the quinoa with a fork and set aside.
- Heat oil in a large non-stick frying pan to a medium-low temperature. Add garlic and spring onions and cook until lightly golden, about 1 minute.
- Add quinoa and cook, stirring occasionally, for 10–12 minutes or until quinoa is lightly golden and slightly crisp around the edges. Season to taste.

Note: This makes about 450 g (1 lb) and, if not serving immediately, cover and store in the refrigerator for up to 3 days.

STEAMED COCONUT AND SPRING ONION BROWN RICE

In its naked state, steamed brown rice can be a bit lacklustre. Infused with spring onions, coconut milk, broth, ginger and a drop of sesame oil, it becomes a dish to swoon over.

INGREDIENTS

200 g (7 oz) long grain brown rice, washed and drained

3 spring onions (scallions), white part only, thinly chopped

½ teaspoon sesame oil

1 cm (½ in) ginger, finely grated

250 ml (8 fl oz) coconut milk

250 ml (8 fl oz) Chicken Broth (p. 187) or stock/broth of choice

pinch of sea salt

METHOD

- Place all the ingredients in a saucepan and bring to the boil.
- Reduce heat to low, cover and simmer until rice is just tender and water has evaporated, about 30–35 minutes. Allow to stand for 5 minutes before serving. Season to taste.

Note: This makes about 600 g (1 lb 5 oz). If you are not serving immediately, cover and store in the refrigerator for up to 3 days.

INDEX

Bacon and egg breakfast ramen 25
Bento bowl with miso glazed salmon,
 edamame and sesame buckwheat 85
Five spice Kentucky fried tofu with
 honey miso slaw 93
Miso butter scallops with watercress
 and soba noodles 58

Mushrooms
Marinated mushrooms with garlic,
 chili and white balsamic vinegar 39
Mushroom and leek quinoa risotto
 with dill pesto 72
Salmon san choy bao 36
Thyme and garlic magic mushrooms
 with poached eggs and
 chimichurri 19
Mushroom and leek quinoa risotto
 with dill pesto 72
My yin and yang bowl with poppy seed-
 crusted sweet potato, lentil and red
 rice salad with creamy tahini
 dressing 89

N
Nanny's self saucing lemon delicious
 pudding 165
No-bake yogurt and mango cheesecake
 pots with cashew coconut crust 174
Nourishing bowl with roasted pumpkin,
 quinoa, chia and mustard
 vinaigrette 76
Nuoc cham 135

Nuts and seeds
Chia Anzac cookies 28
Chunky sticky date pudding granola
 with banana rice cream 27
Cuban mojo chicken bowl with
 roasted radishes, cauliflower cous
 cous and citrus almond dressing 115
Grilled lamb tikka with caramelized
 nectarines and a pinenut and
 pistachio raita 128
Indonesian-style beef gado gado 125
Iranian jewelled rice 141
Israeli chopped salad with scattered
 goat's cheese and almonds 99

Nutty brown rice detox salad with
 blood orange vinaigrette 79
Roasted almond butter 181
Salted almond brittle 162
Seedy superfood crackers 45
Shaved fennel and crushed macadamia
 salad 97
Smoky spiced beef skewers with
 tandoori cashew sauce 120
Soy and balsamic tofu with seedy
 forbidden rice 86
Stuffed turkey with quinoa, cranberry
 and pistachio 143
Thai coconut zucchini noodles with
 prawns and cashews 103
Nut butter, see roasted almond
 butter 181

O

Oats
Chia Anzac cookies 28
Chunky sticky date pudding granola
 with banana nice cream 27
Cinnamon chia oats with banana
 chunks and coconut chips 21
Soaked pineapple and coconut pina
 colada oats 24

P

Parmesan
Parmesan, ricotta and Gruyère sweet
 potato arancini balls with basil
 mayonnaise 35
Kale and almond pesto spaghetti with
 crispy pancetta beans 75
Mushroom and leek quinoa risotto
 with dill pesto 72

Pasta and noodles
Herb and chili turkey mince with
 zucchini noodles and fried egg 127
Kale and almond pesto spaghetti with
 crispy pancetta beans 75
Miso butter scallops with watercress
 and soba noodles 58
Shredded Vietnamese lamb with rice
 noodles and nuoc cham 135

Spicy dan dan noodles with pork and
 chili oil 126
Thai coconut zucchini noodles with
 prawns and cashews 103
Pavlova parfaits with coconut lime cream,
 banana, kiwifruit and passionfruit 168
Peach, white chocolate and macadamia
 tartlets 170
Peanut butter chicken skewers with quick
 bean salad 123
Peking duck breast rice paper rolls with
 plum dipping sauce 138

Pomegranate
Crunchy cauliflower salad with mango,
 lime and jalapeño dressing 100
Sticky pomegranate chicken with
 Iranian jewelled rice 141
Sumac lamb chops with buckwheat,
 crumbled feta and pomegranate 133

Pork
Christmas pork shoulder with chili
 and fennel 134
Spicy dan dan noodles with pork and
 chili oil 126
Stuffed turkey with quinoa, cranberry
 and pistachio 143

Potatoes
Roasted mixed potatoes 157
Salt-and-vinegar potato rösti 152
Smashed baby potatoes with prosciutto
 crackling and dill sour cream
 dressing 148

Prawns
Harissa prawn with charred corn,
 sugar snap pea and beetroot slaw 56
Kaffir lime and chili seafood skewers
 with mango, cucumber and herb
 noodle salad 52
Lemongrass and turmeric seafood
 curry 67
Thai coconut zucchini noodles with
 prawn and cashews 103
Wok fried Japanese bubble and
 squeak with prawns and tamari
 mayonnaise 59

Pumpkin

ACKNOWLEDGEMENTS

With Love

The creation of *Whole Food, Bowl Food* was entirely a family affair. I didn't outsource my recipe testing and editing—it's done entirely in-house and when I say 'in-house', it is literally done in my house. My husband edits my writing and Mum and Dad test all the recipes. Mum cooks, Dad eats … I rely wholeheartedly on my family's generosity and I couldn't have done this without them.

Andrew, my husband and good-humored taste tester, thank you for eating both my culinary successes and failures with dignity and a smile. Mum, thank you for picking up the phone even when you know it's just to run through ideas or help me make recipe decisions (knowing that I will probably ignore your advice anyway). Dad, thank you for not getting too frustrated when Mum is on the phone for hours deciding between almond or hazelnut meal for the chocolate pudding.

To Sam and Kate, Hats, Tom and Will—for graciously accepting all food packages and for your constant interest in my cooking. You are always there for a coffee or prosecco break or a pep talk to keep me motivated.

To all my friends but particularly Katie, Tallulah, Liz, Alex, Nat, Amanda, Tess and Cec for taking part in lengthy food- and recipe-related discussions. I must make a special mention to Judy Whitehead, who is not only the queen of washing up but the calm, rational voice that we needed throughout the photoshoots.

To Diane Ward, who first gave me this incredible opportunity and took me under her wing to publish *Bowl & Fork*, I can't thank you enough. You not only made a dream come true but you've allowed me to keep living my dream. A huge thank you to the entire team at New Holland Publishers and, particularly, Jess McNamara who answers every mundane question and who has logistically made *Whole Food, Bowl Food* possible. To Susie Stevens, who has not only edited both cookbooks but has even road-tested some of the recipes! Thank you for your diligence and kindness.

To our photographer Sue Stubbs and stylist Jane Graystone, it was such a pleasure to collaborate with you. You have brought the recipes to life with such grace and ease, and that is undoubtedly thanks to your talent and professionalism.

A huge thank you to our generous prop suppliers—Rebecca Knight and Sandra McMahon from Weswal Gallery in Tamworth, Country Culture and Angela Lavender.

ABOUT THE AUTHOR

Anna Lisle is a food writer, lifestyle journalist and passionate cook. Her first cookbook *Bowl & Fork* was launched internationally in December 2015.

Anna grew up on a sheep and cattle farm in rural Australia and in 2016 moved to London where she works as a food writer and recipe developer. She is an avid Instagrammer (@annalisle) and blogger (www.annalisle. com), posting recipes and photos which reflect her personal food philosophy of eating natural, wholesome and unprocessed foods.

She has over 10 years' experience working in digital and print media, contributing to various lifestyle platforms.

In 2014 Anna appeared as a contestant on *My Kitchen Rules* together with her mother, Cathy, with their instant restaurant episode attracting 2.25 million viewers. Following their success on the show, Anna and Cathy launched The Walcha Kitchen, a cooking school based at their family property. The Walcha Kitchen also produces a gourmet granola and muesli range that includes paleo and gluten-free options.

www.annalisle.com
@annalisle

First published in 2016 by New Holland Publishers Pty Ltd

London • Sydney • Auckland
The Chandlery, Unit 704, 50 Westminster Bridge Road, London SE1 7QY United Kingdom
1/66 Gibbes Street, Chatswood NSW 2067 Australia
5/39 Woodside Avenue, Northcote, Auckland 0627 New Zealand

www.newhollandpublishers.com

A record of this book is held at the British Library and the National Library of Australia.

ISBN 9781742578910

Managing Director: Fiona Schultz
Publisher: Diane Ward
Project Editor: Susie Stevens
Designer: Lorena Susak
Photographer: Sue Stubbs
Food Stylist: Jane Graystone
Proofreaders: Liz Hardy, Jessica McNamara
Production Director: James Mills-Hicks
Printer: Toppan Leefung Printing Limited

10 9 8 7 6 5 4 3 2 1

Keep up with New Holland Publishers on Facebook
www.facebook.com/NewHollandPublishers